FISCHER&WIESER®
FREDERICKSBURG
FLAVORS

Recipes from the heart of the Texas Hill Country

CASE D. FISCHER & MARK WIESER with JOHN DeMERS

FOOD PHOTOGRAPHY by ANDREW HANENBERG

bright sky press
HOUSTON, TEXAS

I dedicate this book to my lovely wife Deanna
and my three wonderful children – Dietz, Elle and Simon.

– CASE D. FISCHER –

I dedicate this cookbook to my mother, Estella Wieser,
who taught me the value of providing great service and establishing customer
loyalty, and, of course, made those wonderful homemade jams and jellies that
I so often first sampled each summer as she called me to come
to the steps of the back porch to scrape out the last remaining
spoonfuls of each freshly made batch.

– MARK WIESER –

bright sky press
HOUSTON, TEXAS

2365 Rice Boulevard, Suite 202
Houston, Texas 77005

www.brightskypress.com

Library of Congress Cataloging-in-Publication Data on file with publisher.

10 9 8 7 6 5 4 3 2 1

ISBN 978-1-936474-60-8

Editorial Direction, Lucy Herring Chambers
Creative Direction, Ellen Peeples Cregan
Design, Marla Garcia
Printed in Canada through Friesens

contents

our Fredericksburg:
A BRIEF HISTORY

People encountering our little corner of the Lone Star State in that lovely section known as the Hill Country are quick to ask us *who* first settled here. They realize they're looking at something different from towns and cities in other parts of Texas, and they want to know who made Fredericksburg that way. Why, it's Germans, of course—hardly the only ethnic group to sign its name in large letters across the state's history, but certainly one of the most impactful and most progressive. We hope you sense as you walk up and down our clean streets, admire our stone architecture and take in the aromas and flavors of our cuisine, that *we* are what makes Fredericksburg unique.

It's certainly no accident that Germans are so noticeable in Central Texas, for there is strength in numbers. Those who record and quantify such things tell us that Germans were the single largest Texas ethnic group with roots entirely in Europe, making up an impressive five percent of the state's total population throughout the 19th century.

Just as in many parts of the fast-changing United States, the immigration patterns of one group into one area were, above all, the work of one visionary. In a spirit similar to Stephen F. Austin and his "Old 300" families that came to Texas, Germans were by and large lured here by the work and words of Friedrich Dierks, who became famous in the Fatherland as Johann Friedrich Ernst. Hailing with northwestern Germany, Ernst came to America with plans to settle

in Missouri and pursue the horticulture that had supported him back home. In New Orleans, however, he heard of land grants available to Europeans as part of Austin's Texas colony. He applied for and was given 4,000 acres in the northwest corner of today's Austin County, thus forming the heart of the German Belt.

The so-called "America letters" Ernst sent back to Germany influenced thousands who gathered excitedly around the notion of a climate that resembled Sicily more than Germany, where land was fertile and fish and game were abundant, all things needing only the hard work and discipline of good Germans to make the area and its people prosperous. With letters filled with glowing promise—and virtually no mention of the harshness of life here—Ernst attracted a steady stream of Germans to Texas. To *his* part of Texas, where more

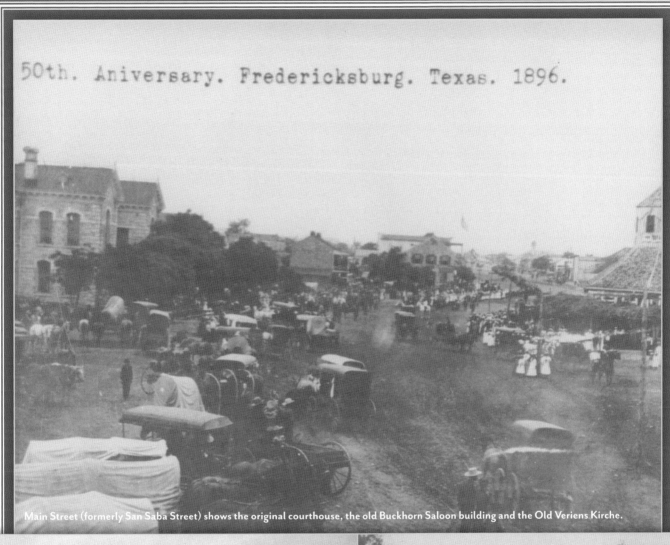

50th. Aniversary. Fredericksburg. Texas. 1896.

Main Street (formerly San Saba Street) shows the original courthouse, the old Buckhorn Saloon building and the Old Veriens Kirche.

A view of Main Street from the Nimitz Hotel.

Early pioneers crossing the Pedernales River.

often than not neighbors had been neighbors in the Old Country. The population of Central Texas grew, drawing mostly from three districts in Germany: Oldenburg, Westphalia and Holstein.

With Ernst essentially doing what today we might call the marketing, Texas seemed ripe for an onslaught of German arrivals by the late 1830s—a fact not lost upon a group of petty noblemen who envisioned a business venture to produce exactly that. Hoping to alleviate overpopulation in rural Germany while enriching themselves, they founded an organization called, depending on what you're reading, Adelsverein, the Verein zum Schutze Deutscher Einwanderer or, with a nod to the new turf, the German Emigration Company. The group followed Ernst's persuasive lead, choosing Texas as the site of their colony. Like so many

similar schemes from Old World to New, the business ended up a disaster but the end result was profound: thousands of German families made their way to central Texas. In three short years, more than seven-thousand Germans turned up in the state, some dropping out due to disease and others lured by the relative big cities of Galveston (the port of entry), Houston and San Antonio. Most, though, made it to the noblemens' Promised land, two towns they'd founded in the Hill Country named New Braunfels and Fredericksburg.

Since all Americans carry mental images of arriving immigrants in the 1800s, it's worth a glance at who and how these Germans were. Generally, they were neither poverty-stricken nor oppressed for reasons of politics or religion. They were solid, middle-class (by the era's definition) farmers and artisans, with no shortage of the

The John Klaerner Saloon is an establishment that would later become the second location of Dietz's bakery which was started by Case's grandfather Theodore Dietz.

very ambition Texas and the rest of the United States clearly needed. A few had education in Germany's universities, and many belonged to families who owned the land they farmed—a dramatic departure from the tenant-farmer norm of most European immigrants. After all, merely signing on to participate in the colony required a substantial cash investment. Later, some might describe that cash as a "barrier to entry." To the Germans, it ended up feeling more like "motivation." And, it's worth noting, that some of the Germans who arrived in Texas were radical free-thinkers, born on that era's incendiary mix of anarchism and socialism. They even included the brother-in-law of one particular German scholar named Karl Marx.

The German Belt, with its twin towns, continued to grow into the 1850s—long after the Adelsverein had trundled off the main stage. There was a lull during the Civil War, thanks to the North's blockade of Confederate ports like Galveston and New Orleans, but arrivals from Germany picked up almost immediately after the South's surrender. By all accounts, most Germans had been sympathetic to the Union anyway, since they'd made their decision on the basis of one, united and growing America.

Fredericksburg itself had been founded by one Baron von (later known as John O.) Meusebach on May 8, 1846, only a year after New Braunfels sixty miles to the southeast, at a spot where two streams came together four miles above the Pedernales River. The idea was to give settlers a way station on their way from New Braunfels to the so-called Fischer-Mueller Grant that started at the Llano River. The settlement's name was chosen to honor Prince Frederick of Prussia.

New arrivals received one lot in town each, along with ten acres of farmland in the vicinity. Modeling Fredericksburg after villages along the Rhine River, the fathers designed a settlement stretching back in neat lines from a wide and comfortable main street—where someday, they figured correctly, commerce would abound. An epidemic in the summer and fall of 1846 killed as many as 150 of the first 1,000 settlers, but those who survived saw advances come to Fredericksburg at a dizzying pace. One of the most striking (and historically important) was the signing of the Meusebach-Comanche Treaty, which eliminated the threat of Indian attack that played such a huge role in the formation of frontier Texas around a series of military outposts. Fredericksburg's peaceful progress was not hindered by such issues, thanks to the treaty. And it would go down in U.S. history as the only agreement between whites and Indians that was never broken. The Comanches even staged a parade down Main Street to celebrate the alliance, and trade flourished between the two populations after that.

Other important achievements within the town's first two years included: the opening of a wagon road between Fredericksburg and Austin; the construction of the Vereins-Kirche, which served for half a century as a church, school, fortress, and meeting hall; the formal organization of Gillespie County by the Texas legislature, with Fredericksburg as its county seat; the construction of the Nimitz Hotel to house travelers; and the U.S. Army's establishment of Fort Martin Scott two miles east of town, which became an important market for the merchants and laborers of Fredericksburg. At that time, Fredericksburg also benefited from being the last town before El Paso on the Emigrant or Upper El Paso Road, making a stop there for rest and supplies almost mandatory. Whatever the weaknesses of their original business scheme, founder John Meusebach and the Adelsverein had chosen their location wisely. During the California Gold Rush of 1849, the town even became an important stop on the popular route.

Perhaps the toughest time many old Fredericksburg families can recall occurred during World War I. After all, here they were, living and thriving as Americans even as Americans went to war against the Kaiser and his Germany. If that weren't suspicious enough, the German settlers of Fredericksburg had invested a good deal of effort in keeping their language and customs alive. While fully half of all German language newspapers in Texas folded during the war, Fredericksburg had a newspaper that continued to print in German well into the 1920s. German Sunday sermons continued into the 1970s, but as a whole World War I cleansed all of America of its German heritage, the most successful transformation in the United States and one led directly by Woodrow Wilson's White House.

The cultural impact of America's great overseas military adventure would be felt for decades. In Fredericksburg—among the town and its families—it either produced or forced residents to cease speaking German in public. The cultural conversion, according to historians, was so profound that relatively little suspicion or animosity remained by the time the U.S. joined the crusade against Adolf Hitler. Forced to choose between cultures by world events they never wanted, the German Americans of Fredericksburg rallied around America. They even sent one of their own, Fleet Admiral Chester Nimitz (whose family had operated the original hotel)

to lead the U.S. naval assault on the forces of Japan—a link to history now commemorated by Fredericksburg's Museum of the Pacific War.

Looking back to the 1960s, it seems that Texas politics and Texas tragedy joined forces to spur Fredericksburg toward the prosperity as a tourist destination it enjoys to this day. International attention was paid on Sunday April 16, 1961, when then-Vice President Lyndon Johnson and Admiral Nimitz helped the first Chancellor of West Germany, Konrad Adenauer to the town for a music festival celebrating ties between the two countries. As many as 10,000 spectators gathered to see (and hear) the speeches and songs, even though the local population at that time was only 4,629. The Austin Recording Company was on hand to tape the *saengerfest* of the program, including Chancellor Adenauer singing with the local children.

> " *Looking back to the 1960s, it seems that Texas politics and Texas tragedy joined forces to spur Fredericksburg toward the prosperity as a tourist destination it enjoys to this day.* "

The Old Nimitz Hotel and saloon, which is now the Admiral Nimitz Museum, before its hallmark spire was constructed. Mark's grandmother, Lena Hahn, cleaned rooms at the hotel before starting her own boarding house.

Just over two years later, when shots rang out in Dallas on Nov. 22, 1963, LBJ became a stunned nation's president—and his ranch in nearby Stonewall became the "Texas White House." All things Texan were America's fascination in the early years of Johnson's administration, until stark differences over civil rights and especially the Vietnam War brought the excitement to an end. By then, however, Fredericksburg has reorganized itself to care for tourists who followed the journalists following LBJ, many of whom considered the Nimitz Hotel their headquarters and the Dietz Bakery (founded by Case's grandfather) one of their favorite stops. Fredericksburg liked what it saw of tourism, apparently, for from that day to this, hotels and bed-and-breakfasts have sprung up any likely place, along with restaurants and shops stretching outward to the town's boundaries and beyond. As always, some locals saw tourism the industry of their future, while others wanted to keep everything just the way it was. In time, visitors would discover in Fredericksburg the perfect blend of small-town quiet and tourist bustle. It is a balance we work hard to keep.

Today, some of Fredericksburg's merchants, seemingly of necessity in modern America, carry the familiar names and logos of the big national chains. Yet there still is, among the rugged Hill Country stone of Fredericksburg's Hauptstrasse and the streets that reach out so neatly from it, the memory of Baron von Meusebach and his first settlers carrying so much promise and progress in their wagons.

two guys *with*
GREAT TASTE BUDS

*l*ong before Fischer & Wieser was a trademark recognized by flavor-crazed foodlovers around the world, Fischer and Wieser were just two guys recognized on the streets of their small, German-founded Texas hometown of Fredericksburg. As far back as 1939, the county boasted at least 32 peach growers, with the Chamber of Commerce encouraging them to band together to spread the gospel of Gillespie County peaches as far away as San Antonio and Austin. In fact, if it hadn't been for Fredericksburg peaches, there probably wouldn't have been a company called Fischer & Wieser at all.

As we'll see in the chapter that follows this one, the culture of hard work and tireless self-improvement that Germans brought to Central Texas was not lost upon two of its sons—men, as it turned out, of two different generations. Even though he made a living as a school teacher and later served as a county judge, Mark could never wander far from memories of his father, a lawyer, bookkeeper and county judge who fancied himself a gentleman farmer. Mark's father immigrated from Germany in 1914, just before the cataclysm of World War I, and settled in Fredericksburg in 1917.

For his part, J.B. Wieser made sure young Mark knew what it was like to grow peaches, apples, plums and wine grapes on the family's land. J.B. was elected vice president of the local Farm Bureau and gave a presentation to its members in 1926 urging them to consider planting fruit trees and eventually opening a processing plant. In fact, Mark offers proudly today, his father wrote a letter and mimeographed it for distribution, specifically suggesting that peaches would be an excellent local crop. Up till then, Mark says, no one knew of the legendary "Fredericksburg peaches" or "Stonewall peaches" from the next town over. Even decades later, peaches were simply a crop his family grew.

"I didn't know anything different at the time," Mark says, remembering the seasonal roadside peach stand he cobbled together from small cedar posts called "stayes" and especially the life-changing day the stand took in $85. "But since I was the last of five kids, I was the last one left to pick our peaches. I watched my mother sort out the peaches and give our customers good-quality measurement. I learned a lot from her. And I realized that people will come back the next year because you

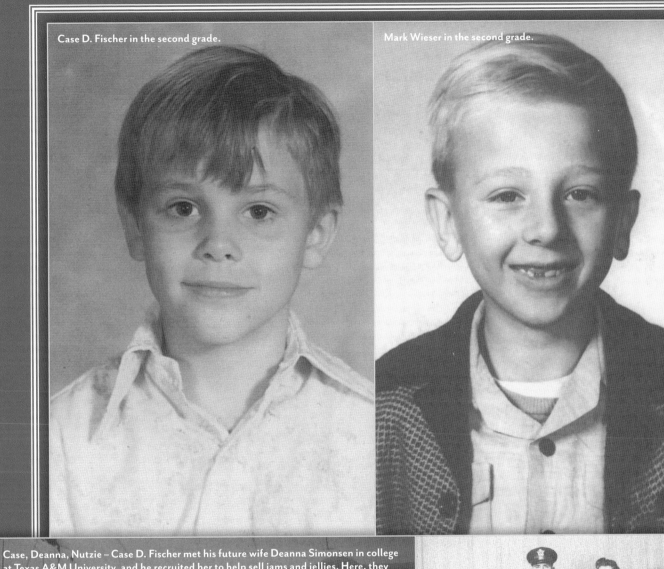

Case D. Fischer in the second grade.

Mark Wieser in the second grade.

Case, Deanna, Nutzie – Case D. Fischer met his future wife Deanna Simonsen in college at Texas A&M University, and he recruited her to help sell jams and jellies. Here, they are working alongside Mark's Aunt Emily Davis Nutzie (Zimmermann) at Oktoberfest.

The Wieser family: Bernice, Estella, Jarvis, Mark, Jeanette, JB and Imogene.

sell them quality things. That really hit home for me back then, and it's still absolutely true."

Mark's father never seriously wanted his son to be a farmer; it was, to his way of thinking, something an intelligent, educated American landowner did on the side of some more impressive "real" profession. It is a mystery, therefore, and one that always makes Mark smile, that one generation of Wieser allowed the next to attend the one university most likely to cause trouble—Texas A&M. Even as he pursued liberal arts studies with a goal of teaching school, Mark found himself profoundly drawn to A&M's world-renowned experimental agriculture. Found *himself*, indeed. Growing things from the soil, and most of all growing things better, became one of the constants of Mark's life—and he never looked at his family's peach trees quite the same way again.

"I had the support of family to expand our orchards to 10,000 trees," he remembers, "and with a high-school friend founded Fredericksburg Orchards with a goal of delivering tree-ripened peaches to area grocers. Unfortunately, we were 30 years too soon as there were no Whole Foods or Central Markets yet, and all grocers wanted was green, rock-hard peaches at 19 cents a pound. California killed the market annually by the end of June, lowering their prices to a point at which we could not recover even processing charges. I grew the trees for three years, and then suffered three years of killing frosts that resulted in no fruit. The seventh year I opened a free Pick-Your-Own and returned to teaching, content to operate a small orchard and sell its production roadside."

Along the way, and somewhat to his surprise, he found he enjoyed being a salesman and that he

Mark Wieser bought this 1870 log cabin in 1967 for $150 to sell peaches off his family's property along Hwy. 87 South. He later added a lean-to for a kitchen, and five years later, he bought the 1913 Lone Star Brewery warehouse, which became Das Peach Haus®.

was pretty good at it. Being friendly, learning how to respond to customer curiosity, and of course how to turn curiosity into a purchase of fresh peaches (or of the old-fashioned peach jellies and preserves his mother made in her home kitchen), all these things were or became the most natural acts in the world to him. Mark liked selling, and he especially loved it as more and more of his customers at the stand were people who'd bought there before.

Mark could have done something like this every summer for the rest of his life. The financial rewards were enough, he figured, especially considering the amount of satisfaction the effort brought him. But what happened next, utterly by chance if you believe in chance, changed everything.

Like all the other peach growers of Gillespie County, Mark Wieser hired local school kids to help with picking—a fact made all the easier in that he was their teacher and, in some cases, their tennis coach. It was a familiar cycle all over farming America, with the local crop coming in just about the time the local schools were letting out. Mark hired whatever kids looked promising, whatever kids wanted to work. There was one kid, though, who did both.

According to company legend, which happens to be true, Case Fischer was a tennis student of Mark's. In fact, the coach remembers him as "the kid always causing trouble on court six." Case clearly had more energy than school, even with a side order of tennis, was able to burn up; so Mark hired him to come help thrash agarita berries. When peaches came in, Case was there to help with that harvest too, all that hot summer long. Case didn't mind any part of the work, no matter how unglamorous, and he kept his eye on

the roadside stand as well. He was intrigued, he now admits, by how selling actually worked. He wasn't actually *in* sales, but he was intrigued by the fact that what you did with a customer, how you treated a customer, had as much to do with making a sale as anything inside the jar, box or basket. True, working with Mark was working with a master. But as the Fischer & Wieser saga would demonstrate, Case was born with some serious mastery of his own.

> **"**
> *and with a high-school friend founded Fredericksburg Orchards with a goal of delivering tree-ripened peaches to area grocers.*
> **"**

As for most kids by this time, high school pointed Case Fischer toward college, and in his family that meant Texas A&M. And as Mark did not have any children of his own, it was not a terrible burden to contribute to Case's courses, studying the very subjects that loomed on the horizon, food science and marketing. Mark understood, from his years of work making and selling food products, that the future (such as he envisioned it at the time) belonged to those who understood these very different but equally important components. Besides, it was Case who first suggested "doing something" with the jams and jellies Mark's mother still made to sell at the stand. You might say Case spent his time at A&M figuring out exactly *what* they were supposed to do.

By 1986, the venture seemed ready to take on a new identity. Das Peach Haus was still what it was, a roadside stand that had grown into a specialty foods store—and that was fine for that single retail location. Yet Case and Mark knew their company had to be bigger, more ambitious and more diversified than any single venue. It was a food company, a manufacturer of not only jams and jellies (their website is still called www.jelly.com) but marinades, condiments, salsas, pasta sauces, and any other specialty food product that made sense at the time. The corporate name they chose, after spending a while as Das Peach Haus Inc., was the simplest one in front of their eyes: Fischer & Wieser. According to Mark, they put "Fischer" first simply because it sounded better.

In a flourish many entrepreneurs will understand, the building of a better mousetrap doesn't exactly mean the world will beat a path to your door—in Fredericksurg, Texas, or anyplace else. No, you have to figure out how to get your mousetrap to the mice. And that Mark and Case did for their first ten years in business, assisted at each step of the journey by Case's wife Deanna. Early on, and to this day, Fischer & Wieser was a family affair—with most of the people likely to answer the phone some relation to the two principals. Case brought in Mark's niece Jenny with a Ph.D. in microbiology—a high school friend of his and then a college friend of Deanna's—to apply more

than taste buds to the company's growing collection of flavor profiles.

"Our goal was and still is that you can find our products anywhere you might think to look for them," Case explains. "When we started, we didn't have any business plan. When you're a small business the way we were, it's really hard to think past the next month and paying the bills. We've just grown the company by finding the next product and the next customer, a little bit at a time." Or, as Mark expresses the same idea; "Had we studied business, had we taken accounting, we would probably not have done this at all!"

We'd had incredible luck, but we've also had a lot of determination. Our success really proved that if you're willing to ride out the low spots, it can start looking really good."

The journey was one that was (and is) the food industry's answer to the unheralded rock band playing any gig it could get, and driving all night to get there. And with food companies, as with rock bands, the rest of the world only cares if the efforts pay off. In the case

> **"**
> *Our goal was and still is that you can find our products anywhere you might think to look for them.*
> **"**

Case & Mark accepting NASFT Gold sofi™ in 2010 for Mom's Pasta Sauce Outstanding Classic in New York.

Case D. Fischer proudly holds the NASFT Gold sofi™ award for Fischer & Wieser's flagship product, The Original Roasted Raspberry Chipotle Sauce®. It won Outstanding New Product in 1997.

Fischer & Wieser friends and team members at the 2010 Fancy Food Show receive the award for Mom's Pasta Outstanding Classic. From left to right are Deanna and Case D. Fischer, Simon Fischer, Dietz Fischer, Elle Fischer, Jay Gans, Lauren Cone, Caroline Cone, Mark Wieser, Martha Major, Yvonne Fox and Jonathan Pehl.

of Fischer & Wieser offering food products, the partners understood intuitively that everything was riding on flavor. Hailing from Texas, where German influences were never far from Mexican, Case and Mark had a natural flair for making things that tasted great. But how would anybody ever know? Answer: the guys went anywhere anybody let them, giving out free samples.

With 20/20 hindsight, we might say Fischer & Wieser built its fan base one set of taste buds at a time. They hardly missed a church social or county fair, slowly building to the point of having booths at regional and then national food shows. "Hi, we're Fischer & Wieser from Fredericksburg, Texas, would you like to taste our great new sauce?" may not be quite perfect as grammar or punctuation, but it must have become the single sentence that haunted their dreams night after night. The world did taste, and the world loved what it tasted. Though it took that first decade, the products eventually won enough awards and reviews to attract a network of food brokers and distributors to get the ever-growing line onto the nation's supermarket shelves.

Over the years since 1986, starting early and intensifying later, Case and Mark found that the business they were in never stopped evolving with their success. For instance, like the preserving of produce throughout the ages, the jellies and related items they began with were a way of extending the life of a perishable product beyond the peak of its season. It took almost no time, though, for consumer demand to outstrip the ability of the Wieser land to produce enough, thus inspiring the partners to buy from many local farm families. The business links to these families grew as deep and tangled as their personal histories.

With success also comes attention from other companies, for a variety of reasons. While some entities simply want to sell you something, others see ways that you might want to help them out, that you might actually be the guys to run their business better than they can run it themselves. So it was that Patrick Timpone (now an Austin natural foods expert) approached Case and Mark in 2001 to take over all phases of making and selling his mother's pasta sauces. Nenfa Timpone for years had prepared her "fast sauce" and other variations for Patrick to enjoy, an authentic home-cooking process that still includes first-rate California tomatoes, whole cloves of garlic and basil leaves from the Texas town of Blanco. Mom's pasta sauces—that's their official name—have been a hit ever since.

Case also found himself employing (and enjoying!) many hours in the company test kitchen. As both partners remember thousands of people at trade shows liking a new product but then asking "What can I do with it?", Case took it upon himself to come up with some compelling answers. Pouring a sauce over cream cheese was one of the earliest and most successful suggestions, especially when applied to Fischer & Wieser's 1015 Onion Jelly (the 1015 sweet onion being one of the many items developed at Texas A&M). Still, despite an enthusiastic reception for what they dubbed "the national hors d'oeuvre of Texas," Case wasn't satisfied. He kept on experimenting with other flavors.

In one of American food history's great "Eureka!" moments, Case hit upon the notion of mixing a then-little-known smoke-dried chile pepper with raspberries to produce a sauce that was every Texans' fantasy of sweet-meets-smoky. What came to be known as The Original Roasted Raspberry *Chipotle* Sauce® (especially after it inspired dozens of imitators) was given out that year at Fredericksburg's Oktoberfest celebration. Everybody who tasted the sauce—of course, poured over cream cheese—had to buy a bottle or two. In 1997, the creation won the gold medal from the NASFT, and it has continued to bring home first-places from shows and grocery chains ever since. Fischer & Wieser's single best-known product is now considered a major factor in the broader popularity of chipotle.

To this day, the test kitchen strikes many as the heart of Fischer and Wieser. The business partners still do a variety of research with an eye on the future, from attending trade shows across America as well as in Europe to reading anything published in industry magazine about taste trends. The result is a kind of freeform, utterly unmapped adventure through countries and regions, ethnicities and cultures, in search of the Next Big Thing. Being Case and Mark, even more than they are Fischer & Wieser, they not only feed the employees with experiments good, bad or indifferent but they actively listen to what anybody who's tasting has to say.

"When you have a company made up of foodies, it's really fun to get in the test kitchen," Case says. "There's not a lot of rocket science involved, even if it takes months, even if it takes ten, fifteen or twenty times till you get the flavor perfect and it just says 'Wow!' Whenever people try a great product, they'll embrace it." Case ponders a moment, then decides to offer his summary of the past twenty-five-plus years. "Our goal is to inspire your culinary adventure. All you have to do is get in there and stretch the boundaries of flavor."

Peach trees are in full bloom in the spring of 2012 as Case D. Fischer and Mark Wieser inspect the foliage.

FISCHER & WIESER.

RECIPES

appetizers

BEST *seven* LAYER *dip in* TEXAS!

3 medium avocados – peeled, pitted and diced

⅜ cup Fischer & Wieser Guacamole Starter–Just Add Avocados

¼ cup chopped fresh cilantro

Garlic salt to taste

Ground black pepper to taste

1 (8 ounce) container sour cream

1 (1 ounce) package taco seasoning mix

1 (16 ounce) can refried beans

¼ cup Fischer & Wieser Salsa a La Charra Salsa

4 roma (plum) tomatoes, diced

1 bunch green onions, finely chopped

2 cups shredded Mexican-style cheese blend

1 (2.25 ounce) can black olives – drained and finely chopped

Large bag tortilla chips

Here in the Lone Star State, people never make enemies by bringing something to dip tortilla chips in. Try this easy, quick-to-fix appetizer for your next family gathering or covered dish get-together.

In a medium bowl, mash the avocados. Mix in Fischer & Wieser Guacamole Starter–Just Add Avocados, cilantro, garlic salt and pepper. In a small bowl, blend the sour cream and taco seasoning. In a 9" x 13" dish or on a large serving platter, spread the refried beans. Top with sour cream mixture, then Fischer & Wieser Salsa a la Charra Salsa. Spread on guacamole. Top with tomatoes, green onions, Mexican-style cheese blend and black olives. Serve with tortilla chips or crackers of your choice. Serves 12 as appetizer.

STUFFED *jalapeños*

1 (8 ounce) block cream cheese, softened

2 finely chopped green onions, including tops

½ cup finely chopped pecans

¼ cup Fischer & Wieser Mild Green or Red Hot Jalapeño Jelly

12–18 pickled jalapeños, sliced in half lengthwise and seeded

These stuffed hot peppers—some hotter than others, as your mouth has probably discovered by now—are a treat for football get-togethers, card parties, or summer cookouts. They even invite a contest, to see who can eat the most.

Mix cream cheese, green onions, chopped pecans, and Fischer & Wieser Mild Green or Red Hot Jalapeño Jelly until well-blended. Fill jalapeño halves with mixture. Place on serving platter and watch them disappear! Serves 4–6

SWEET ONION *& garlic dip*

1 (8 ounce) block cream cheese, softened

¾ cup Fischer & Wieser Sweet Onion and Garlic Marmalade

¼ cup chopped green onions

1 (4 ounce) can chopped black olives

½ cup chopped pecans

Try this as a dip with crackers or chips, or a spread on variety breads to accompany a cold cut tray at your next event.

Mix cream cheese and Fischer & Wieser Sweet Onion and Garlic Marmalade until well blended. Add chopped green onions, black olives, and chopped pecans. If desired, roll in chopped pecans. Serves 8–12

SWEET ONION & GARLIC DIP

!ESPECIAL! *pasilla* CHILE *finishing sauce* CON QUESO DIP

1 pound easy melt cheese, cut into small chunks

½ cup onion, finely chopped

1¼ cups Fischer & Wieser Salsa a la Charra

½ cup Fischer & Wieser !Especial! Pasilla Chile Finishing Sauce

Large bag tortilla chips

Gooey, drippy, spicy queso is a Texas party standard. Serve it in a chafing dish or slow cooker with some good corn tortilla chips. Our version, with Fischer & Wieser Gourmet !Especial! Pasilla Chile Finishing Sauce, takes the flavor of the dip to a whole other level.

Combine all ingredients in a slow cooker set on low. Cook, stirring often, until cheese has melted and mixture is creamy. Continue to cook for 20 more minutes. Serve hot with tortilla chips. 16 (¼ cup) servings.

HOT *habanero salsa* GUACAMOLE

4 ripe Haas avocados, peeled, pitted and roughly chopped

1 tablespoon fresh cilantro, minced

½ cup Fischer & Wieser Hot Habanero Salsa

Sea salt to taste

1 bag corn tortilla chips

Some like it hot! And if you apply that notion to your guacamole, you need to try it with our Fischer & Wieser Hot Habanero Salsa!

Combine all ingredients except salt in food processor fitted with steel blade. Process to desired consistency. Transfer to a bowl and season to taste with sea salt. Serve with corn tortilla chips. Serves 6.

FISCHER & WIESER *four star* BLACK RASPBERRY CHIPOTLE *sauce* OVER WARM *brie cheese*

This is a positively divine finger food. Combine the sultry, musky tang of a good brie cheese with the slightly tart sweetness of fresh black raspberries and throw in a subtle chipotle chile heat—how could it not be wonderful?

8 ounce wedge of 60% brie cheese

1 cup Fischer & Wieser Four Star Black Raspberry Chipotle Sauce

Mint sprig as garnish

Wheat Thins crackers, or your favorite whole grain cracker

Preheat oven to 350° F. Using a sharp paring knife, remove the rind from the wedge of brie. Place the cheese on a heatproof serving platter and cook in preheated oven until the cheese has just begun to soften and ooze, about 10 minutes. Remove platter from oven using pot holders. Pour the Fischer & Wieser Four Star Black Raspberry Chipotle Sauce over the cheese, allowing it to spill over the sides of the wedge. Garnish platter with mint sprig and serve alongside a basket of crackers. Serves 6–8 as finger food.

JOHN'S *smoked* RASPBERRY *chipotle* BARBECUED *meatballs*

2 pounds lean ground beef

1 cup dry breadcrumbs

2/3 cup finely chopped onion

½ cup milk

2 tablespoons chopped fresh parsley

2 teaspoons salt

1 teaspoon Worcestershire sauce

⅛ teaspoon black pepper

2 eggs

1½ cups Fischer & Wieser's The Original Roasted Raspberry Chipotle Sauce®

1½ cups prepared barbecue sauce

3 tablespoons prepared ketchup

2 tablespoons prepared yellow mustard

2 tablespoons cider vinegar

Years before this book was a glimmer in anyone's eye, John DeMers was wowing his friends with this application of Fischer & Wieser's most famous sauce. "Bring those meatballs" became a common refrain, whenever anyone he knew threw a party. What better venue than this to share what might be the best cocktail meatballs you'll ever taste?

Heat oven to 400° F. In a large mixing bowl, combine beef, breadcrumbs, onion, milk, parsley, salt, Worcestershire, pepper and eggs. Shape into small (1 inch) meatballs. Place in ungreased rectangular pan, or on rack in broiler pan. Bake uncovered about 20 minutes, until no longer pink in center and juice is clear.

While meatballs are cooking, prepare the sauce in a pan large enough to also hold the meatballs over medium heat. Combine all remaining ingredients and bring to a boil, then reduce heat and let simmer. When meatballs are cooked, drain them of fat and transfer them to the sauce, letting them simmer for 30 minutes. Serve hot in a chafing dish with toothpicks. Serves 6.

SOUP *bone* CATTLE COMPANY'S WILDSEED FARMS* *biscuits*

2 cups of Pioneer or other all-purpose flour

1 tablespoon baking powder

½ teaspoon salt

1 teaspoon coarsely ground black pepper

⅓ cup butter

¾ cup whole milk

4 ounces shredded cheddar cheese

½ stick (¼ cup) butter

* 100 Legacy Drive
800.848.0078
www.wildseedfarms.com

Wildseed Farms is a must-visit for any avid gardeners passing anywhere near Fredericksburg, and there are some nice, light lunches served there too. Still, if you ask the employees, the biggest food thrill is any day Soup Bone Cattle Company stops by to make biscuits the old-fashioned cowboy way—in a Dutch oven buried in the ground with hot coals.

Preheat oven to 400° F. Combine flour, baking powder, salt and pepper, and mix well. Add butter and work in until mixture resembles cornmeal. Add milk and cheese; mix into a tacky ball. Spread a small portion of flour on board and knead until spongy. Press out with hands or roll out. Cut individual biscuits with a biscuit-cutter dusted with flour. Place biscuits tight to each other; this will make them rise rather than spread. Place lid on Dutch oven. Line the outside of your Dutch oven lid with coals then add three more to the lid. Count the coals and put ½ as many coals on bottom of oven. Remember ⅔ coals on top and ⅓ on the bottom. Cook in oven or in coals in ground for 15–20 minutes, until golden brown. Serves 8–10.

THE ORIGINAL *roasted raspberry* CHIPOTLE SAUCE® *&* CREAM CHEESE *appetizer*

1 (3 ounce) package cream cheese

⅓ cup Fischer & Wieser's The Original Roasted Raspberry Chipotle Sauce®

Fresh raspberries and mint for garnish, if desired

Gingersnap cookies or assorted crackers

If you can think of an easier, more elegant and delicious appetizer, bring it on. With just a twist of the wrist, this show-stopping recipe can be ready to serve in less than a minute.

Place cream cheese on serving dish and pour ⅓ cup The Original Roasted Raspberry Chipotle Sauce® over top, allowing it to drizzle down sides of cream cheese. Garnish with fresh raspberries and mint, if desired. Serve with gingersnap cookies or assorted crackers. Serves 2.

NOTE: For an 8 ounce package of cream cheese, use ½–¾ cup of sauce.

TIP: Whip cream cheese with sauce (using measurements above). Form into a ball, and roll in chopped pistachio nuts or chopped, toasted pecans. Sprinkle parsley on top or drizzle with two tablespoons of additional sauce. Serve with gingersnap cookies or assorted crackers.

appetizers

FISCHER & WIESER *queso* DIP

1 pound pasteurized processed cheese, cut into small chunks

1 cup Fischer & Wieser Queso Starter–Just Add Cheese

1 (12 ounce or larger) bag tortilla chips

Here's another version of the queso dip so popular in every corner of Texas. And this product makes queso so easy, it gives the directions right in its name.

Combine all ingredients in a slow cooker set on low. Cook, stirring often, until cheese has melted and mixture is creamy. Leave in slow cooker to serve; serve hot with tortilla chips. Serves 8.

BLACKBERRY *la Bamba* SALSA

2 cups canned mandarin orange segments, well drained and roughly chopped

1 small red onion, finely diced

1 cup Fischer & Wieser Roasted Blackberry Chipotle Sauce

⅓ cup freshly squeezed lime juice

1 bunch cilantro, leaves and tender stems, chopped

1 bag corn tortilla chips

If you like our Raspberry Rumba Salsa, you'll love this "La Bamba" variation. The Fischer & Wieser Roasted Blackberry Chipotle Sauce adds a rich, subtly sweet and smoky flavor that transcends even luscious.

Combine all ingredients in a medium sized bowl and stir to blend well. Refrigerate until ready to serve. Turn salsa out into serving bowl and serve alongside a basket of corn tortilla chips. Yield: 3½ cups.

RASPBERRY RUMBA *salsa*

2 cups canned Mandarin orange segments, well drained and roughly chopped

1 small red onion, cut into tiny diced bits

1 cup Fischer & Wieser The Original Roasted Raspberry Chipotle Sauce®

⅓ cup freshly squeezed lime juice

1 bunch cilantro, leaves and tender stems chopped

1 bag corn tortilla chips

If you and your friends love both texture and a bit of citrus zing in their salsa, this should be a big hit at your next party.

Combine all ingredients in a medium sized bowl and stir to blend well. Refrigerate until ready to serve. Turn salsa out into serving bowl and serve alongside a basket of corn tortilla chips. Yields 3½ cups.

MOM'S SPINACH *and* artichoke **DIP**

Want a very special, Italian-flavored hot appetizer that everyone will rave about? This one built around the classic combination of spinach and artichoke should make you happy indeed.

½ cup butter

½ onion finely chopped

1 package frozen spinach, thawed

1 (8 ounce) package cream cheese

1 (8 ounce) package sour cream

¾ cup shredded asiago cheese

1 jar marinated artichokes, chopped

Red pepper flakes to taste

2 cups bread crumbs

1 cup Mom's Artichoke & Asiago Pasta Sauce

8 ounces shredded Monterey Jack cheese

Saute the onions in butter, adding spinach, cream cheese, sour cream, shredded asiago cheese, marinated artichokes, red pepper flakes, bread crumbs, and Mom's Artichoke and Asiago Pasta Sauce, while mixing and blending well after each addition. Remove from heat and put in crocks or microwave dish. Top with Monterey Jack cheese and melt. Serve hot with chips or bread. Serves 14–16.

The Fischer family are on the Texas A&M University campus, seated from left are Deanna and Elle, and standing are Simon, Case and Dietz.

Fischer & Wieser Chief Operating Officer Jenny Wieser, Ph.D., was honored by the Fredericksburg Chamber of Commerce in 2012 as Business Woman of the Year. She stands embraced by the proud arms of husband Terry and their son Jack.

Simon Fischer and his mother Deanna take a moment to pose for a picture at the 2012 Nimitz Golf Classic, a tournament Fischer & Wieser proudly sponsored and served sandwiches with their prized sauces.

The Fischer and Wieser families gather together on the peach orchard that started it all. From left are Case D. and Deanna Fischer, Simon Fischer, Jack Wieser and Elle Fischer (in the tractor seat), Dietz Fischer (seated), Terry, Jenny Wieser and Mark Wieser.

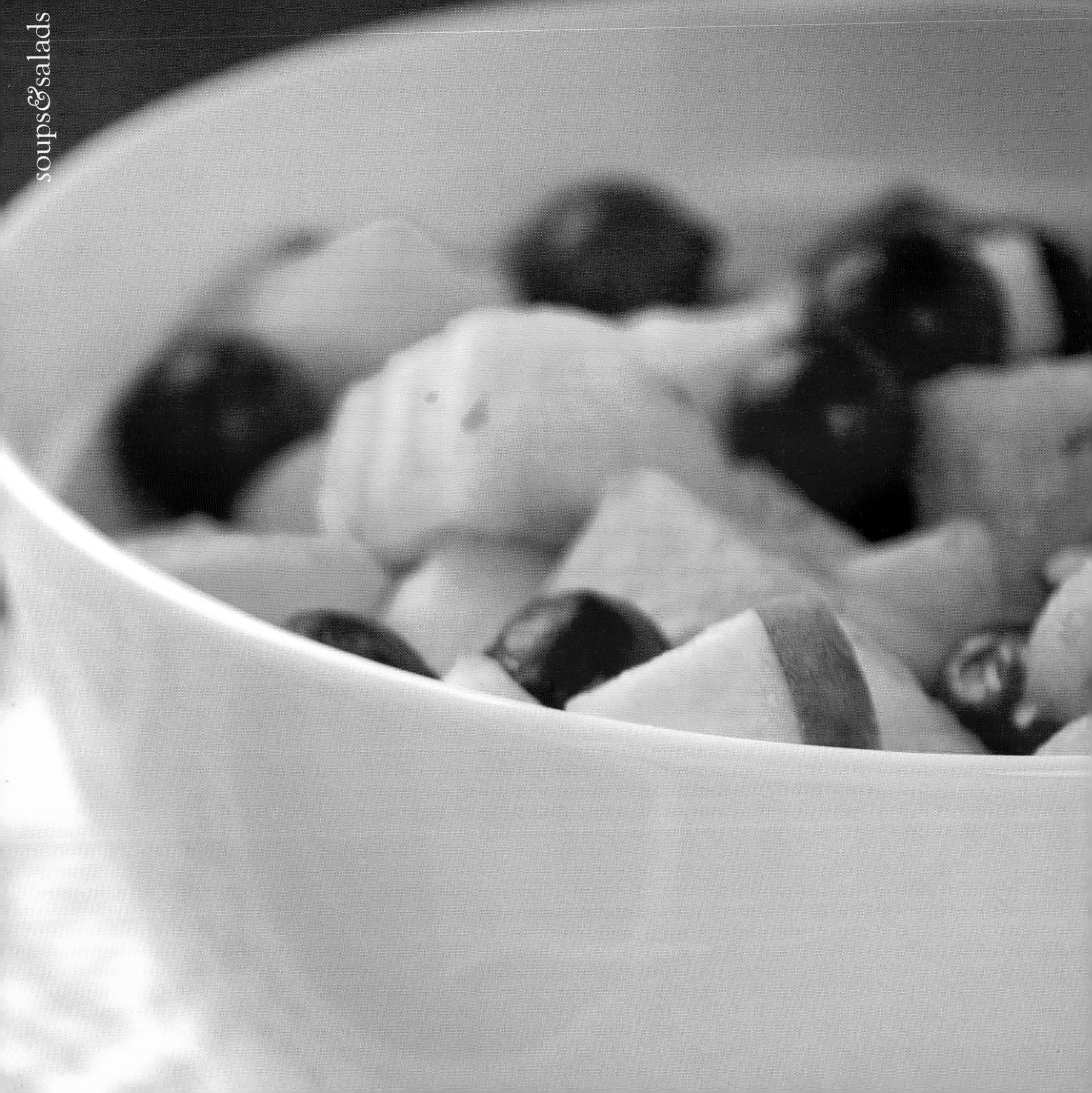

RECIPES

soups&salads

CHICKEN *tortilla* SOUP
a la CHARRA

2 tablespoons olive oil

2 yellow onions, chopped

2 large carrots, finely chopped

1 tablespoon minced garlic

1 roasted chicken, bones and skin removed, meat cut into bite-sized pieces

8 cups chicken broth

2 cups Fischer & Wieser Salsa a la Charra

½ cup freshly squeezed lime juice, plus additional

¼ cup plus ¼ cup chopped cilantro leaves

1 tablespoon chopped jalapeño, or to taste

½ teaspoon garlic powder

½ teaspoon onion powder

Salt and black pepper to taste

1 tomato, chopped

2 avocados, chopped

½ cup grated cheddar or jack cheese

Showcasing the deep flavor of roasted tomatoes in our salsa, this version of classic Tex-Mex tortilla soup is a winner any time of year. After all, it's a bit on the spicy side, and people in hot climates always say that cools you down.

Saute the onions and carrots until they begin to caramelize, then add the garlic for a couple of quick stirs, just enough to release its flavor. Stir in the pieces of chicken, combining. Add the chicken broth, followed by the salsa and lime juice. Bring to a quick boil, then reduce heat to a simmer. Add the chopped cilantro and season with jalapeño, garlic and onion powders, and salt and pepper. Simmer for about 30 minutes so flavors can meld. When ready to serve, ladle the soup into large bowls and garnish with remaining cilantro, tomato, avocado and cheese. Splash with additional lime juice, if desired. Serves 8–10.

MEXICALI *cheese soup* WITH FISCHER & WIESER *chipotle & corn* SALSA

1 quart chicken broth

2 teaspoons chili powder

1 pound pasteurized processed cheese, cut into 1 inch cubes

2 cups Fischer & Wieser Chipotle & Corn Salsa

1 tablespoon cornstarch mixed with 1½ tablespoons water

Salt to taste

Chopped cilantro as garnish

Craving a hearty cheese soup on a cold winter evening? This one, prepared with Fischer & Wieser's Chipotle & Corn Salsa, will satisfy your craving and then some. It's so easy you'll want to keep the ingredients on hand just in case company comes by.

Combine chicken broth, chili powder and pasteurized processed cheese in a heavy 6 quart soup pot over medium heat. Cook, stirring occasionally, until cheese has melted, about 15 minutes. Add the Fischer & Wieser Chipotle & Corn Salsa and bring to a boil. Add the cornstarch mixture, stirring constantly, and cook just until soup thickens slightly. Remove from heat and add salt to taste. Serve hot, garnished with minced cilantro. Serves 6–8.

NOTE: To make the soup even heartier, add chunks of leftover chicken, turkey, ham or crisply cooked crumbled bacon before adding cornstarch mixture; allow to heat 5 minutes, then add cornstarch mixture and proceed as directed.

SOUTHWESTERN *cheese soup* with FISCHER & WIESER *queso starter–just add* CHEESE

1 quart chicken broth

2 teaspoons chili powder

1 pound pasteurized process cheese, cut into 1 inch cubes

2 cups Fischer & Wieser Queso Starter–Just Add Cheese

1 tablespoon cornstarch mixed with 1½ tablespoons water

Salt to taste

Minced cilantro as garnish

Fischer & Wieser Queso Starter–Just Add Cheese will satisfy your craving. Even in Texas, winters get cold enough for us to need a soup like this. Or at least we can always run the air conditioner.

Combine chicken broth, chili powder and diced pasteurized processed cheese in a heavy 6 quart soup pot over medium heat. Cook, stirring occasionally, until cheese has melted, about 15 minutes. Add the Fischer & Wieser Queso Starter–Just Add Cheese and bring to a boil. Add the cornstarch mixture, stirring constantly, and cook just until soup thickens slightly. Remove from heat and add salt to taste. Serve hot, garnished with minced cilantro. Serves 6–8.

TOMATO BASIL *soup* SHRIMP *& rice* GUMBO

½ medium onion, chopped

2 cups cooked frozen shrimp, chopped (may substitute sausage or chicken for shrimp if desired)

2 tablespoons melted butter or olive oil

1 cup Mom's Limited Edition Tomato Basil Soup

1 tsp Cajun Seasoning, if desired

2 cups cooked rice

Sometimes two great dishes—like tomato basil soup and shrimp and rice gumbo—find they make an even better soup when they're combined.

Saute onion and shrimp in melted butter or olive oil. Add Mom's Limited Edition Tomato Basil Soup and Cajun Seasoning. Bring to boil; lower heat to simmer; simmer 10–15 minutes. Cook rice according to directions on package. Serve shrimp sauce over rice. Serves 4.

DAS PEACH HAUS *peach salsa* GAZPACHO

4 white corn tortillas

Canola oil for frying

Salt

4 cups Fischer & Wieser Das Peach Haus® Peach Salsa, well chilled

1 cup sour cream

¼ cup minced cilantro

Here's a great chilled soup that is ready in a flash. Prepare the tortilla strips ahead of time and you have a wonderful soup in ten minutes!

Place the tortillas in a stack. Using a sharp knife, cut the stack in half, then stack the cut halves together. Cut the tortillas into ¼ inch wide strips. Heat the oil to 350° F and fry the tortilla strips until golden brown, about 3 minutes. Remove with a slotted spoon and drain on absorbent paper towels. Toss with salt to season. Pour the chilled salsa into blender and puree until smooth. To serve, pour 1 cup of the pureed salsa into four shallow soup plates (clear glass looks great!). Place two tablespoons of the sour cream in the center of each serving. Scatter some of the tortilla strips over the sour cream. Garnish each bowl with 1 tablespoon of the minced cilantro, scattering it over the entire bowl. Serve at once and enjoy a refreshing cool breeze in a bowl. Serves 4.

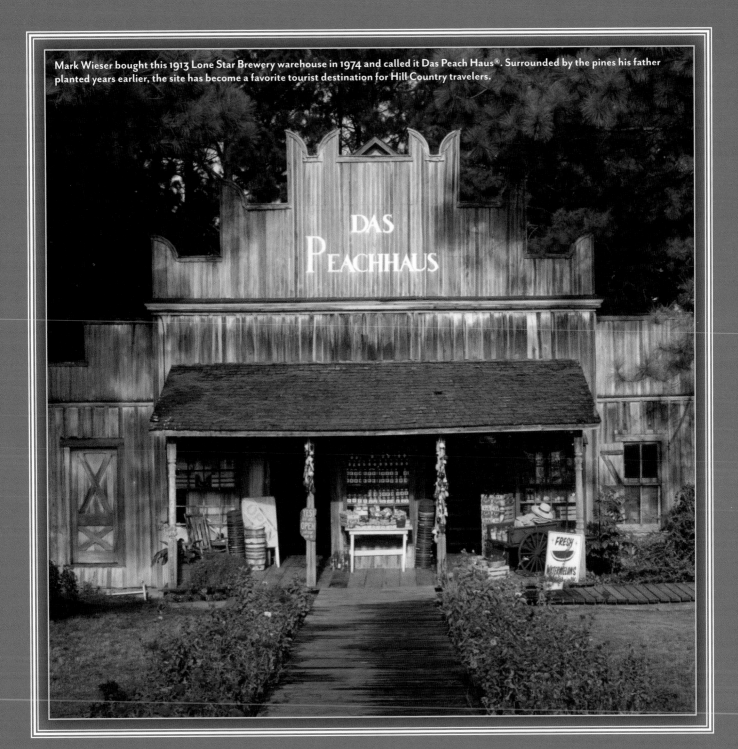

Mark Wieser bought this 1913 Lone Star Brewery warehouse in 1974 and called it Das Peach Haus®. Surrounded by the pines his father planted years earlier, the site has become a favorite tourist destination for Hill Country travelers.

TACO *soup*

1 pound ground beef, browned and drained (or ground turkey)

½ medium onion, chopped

3 cups Timpone's Salsa Muy Rica

1 can whole yellow corn or hominy, undrained

1 can red or black beans, undrained

1 package Original Ranch Style Dressing Mix

1 package taco seasoning (mild or hot, as desired)

GARNISH:

Grated cheddar or Monterey Jack cheese

Tortilla chips

Sour cream

Avocado slices

Black olives

Jalapeños

The flavors of a terrific taco—and you know how much we all love and crave those—come together in this soup that's a satisfying meal all by itself.

Brown ground beef or turkey and onions in skillet. Drain. Place ground beef or turkey and onions, Timpone's Salsa Muy Rica, corn or hominy, red or black beans, Ranch Dressing Mix, and taco seasoning mix in Dutch oven (or add to skillet if size permits). Simmer 30 minutes or longer, as desired. Serve with garnishes of your choice. Serves 8.

CHEDDAR *ale soup* FROM *Fredericksburg* BREWING CO.*

4 cups diced celery

4 cups shredded carrots

2 ounces butter

½ cup flour

8 cups chicken broth

1 cup Fredericksburg Brewing Co. Enchanted Rock Red Ale

36 ounce pasteurized processed cheese

2½ pounds shredded cheddar cheese

Green onion for garnish

* 245 East Main Street
830.997.1946
www.yourbrewery.com

Already blessed with so many wineries, Fredericksburg is really proud to have its very own brewpub. This soup recipe is wildly popular there—especially since it pairs perfectly with one or more glasses of the red ale in the recipe.

Cook celery and carrots with butter. Add flour for thickening. Add chicken broth and beer then bring to a boil. Slowly add pasteurized processed cheese then slowly sprinkle in shredded cheddar cheese, whisking it for smoothness (important to whisk when adding cheddar or the soup will get clumpy). Garnish with green onion. Makes about 2 quarts.

MEXICAN *meatball soup* *with* BLACK BEANS *and* CORN

2 tablespoons olive oil

2 small onions (2 cups), diced

5 garlic cloves, minced (divided)

2 bay leaves

5 (14.5 ounce) cans beef broth

1 (16 ounce) jar Fischer & Wieser Black Bean and Corn Salsa)

½ cup chopped fresh cilantro (divided)

1 pound lean ground beef

¼ pound bulk pork sausage

6 tablespoons yellow cornmeal

¼ cup milk

1 large egg

½ teaspoon salt

½ teaspoon ground black pepper

½ teaspoon ground cumin

½ cup long-grain white rice

Here's a traditional soup that just gets better with the addition of two staples of the Americas, black beans and corn. And since there's rice involved, this is a soup than can satisfy just about anybody as a full meal.

Heat oil in a heavy pot over medium-high heat. Add onion, 3 garlic gloves and bay leaves; saute 5 minutes. Add broth, salsa and ¼ cup cilantro; bring to a boil. Cover and simmer 15 minutes. Meanwhile, combine ground beef, pork sausage, cornmeal, milk, egg, salt, pepper, cumin, 2 garlic gloves and ¼ cup cilantro in medium bowl. Mix well. Shape meat mixture by generous tablespoonfuls into 1 to 1¼ inch balls.

Add rice and meatballs to soup and bring to a boil, stirring occasionally. Reduce heat; cover and simmer until rice and meatballs are tender, stirring occasionally, about 20 minutes. Season to taste with salt and pepper. Ladle soup into bowls and serve. Makes 8 servings.

BLUEBERRY *chipotle* *melon* SALAD

⅔ cup Fischer & Wieser Roasted Blueberry Chipotle Sauce

⅓ cup fresh orange juice

2 tablespoons dry sherry

⅔ cup crème fraiche

2 teaspoons minced fresh mint

2½ cups cubed fresh cantaloupe

2½ cups cubed fresh honeydew melon

Green leaf lettuce leaves and mint sprigs as garnish

Toss melons in crème fraiche, sherry, mint and orange juice and you've got a sure bet for a delightfully different, refreshing summer salad. Especially when you add our Fischer & Wieser's Roasted Blueberry Chipotle Sauce.

Combine the Fischer & Wieser Roasted Blueberry Chipotle Sauce, orange juice, sherry, crème fraiche and mint in a medium-sized bowl; whisk to blend well. Stir in the melon cubes; stir to coat well. Refrigerate until ready to serve. To serve, place a lettuce leaf on each serving plate and top with a portion of the salad. Garnish with mint sprigs. Serves 4.

HARVEST *apple* CIDER *cole* SLAW

It's quick and easy, but this cole slaw definitely stands out from the ordinary picnic accompaniments. You better get your recipe card ready for sharing.

2 tablespoons red wine vinegar

1½ cups real mayonnaise

2 tablespoons Fischer & Wieser Harvest Apple Cider Glaze

½ teaspoon ground red pepper

1 teaspoon freshly ground black pepper

1 (16 ounce) package shredded coleslaw mix with carrots and red cabbage

4 green onions, thinly sliced, including green tops

Mix together the vinegar, mayonnaise and the Fischer & Wieser Harvest Apple Cider Glaze. Using a whisk mix thoroughly then add the ground red pepper and black pepper, adjusting as necessary for taste, and also mixing throughout. Next add all the slaw ingredients and toss to coat completely. Place in a covered bowl and let marinate in refrigerator 2–3 hours before serving. Serves 6–10.

HARVEST *apple* GLAZE *ham* SALAD

2 pounds smoked ham, cut into rough cubes

1 onion, finely chopped

2 celery stalks, finely chopped

6 hard-boiled eggs, chopped

⅓ cup chopped smoked almonds

1 tablespoon dried oregano

1 teaspoon salt

1 teaspoon freshly ground black pepper

1½ cups Fischer & Wieser Harvest Apple Cider Glaze

1 cup real mayonnaise

2 tablespoons minced cilantro

Use your leftover ham to make this tasty salad. It's great for sandwiches with sliced gruyere cheese, or pile the salad on leaf lettuce leaves for an entree salad.

Place the ham cubes in work bowl of food processor fitted with steel blade; process until ground to the consistency of ground beef. Transfer to a bowl and stir in the onion, celery, chopped eggs and almonds; set aside. In a separate bowl, whisk together remaining ingredients, blending well. Fold the dressing into the ham mixture. Refrigerate until ready to use. Serves 4–6.

THE CO-PILOT *sandwich* *from* AIRPORT DINER*

8 boiled chicken breasts

1 cup diced celery

1 small yellow onion, diced

1½ teaspoon chopped tarragon

1½ tablespoon chopped parsley

1 cup mayonnaise

3 teaspoons lemon juice

2 teaspoons Dijon mustard

2 teaspoons salt

1 teaspoon black pepper

* 155 Airport Road
830.997.4999
www.airportdiner.com

At Fredericksburg Airport, there's a striking, aviation-themed place to stay called the Hanger Hotel. And a popular part of that property is the aviation-meets-1950s eatery called the Airport Diner. This is their tarragon-kissed version of the all-American chicken salad sandwich.

Chop up boiled chicken and mix with all other ingredients in a bowl. Serve with lettuce and tomato on toasted bread (sourdough is always one of our favorite options). Serves 8–10.

POMEGRANATE *& mango* *chipotle* CHICKEN SALAD

SALAD:

2 pounds roasted chicken, skinned and cut into rough cubes

1 onion, finely chopped

2 celery stalks, finely chopped

2 roasted red bell peppers, chopped

1 cup corn kernels, roasted

1 cup pecans or walnuts, chopped

DRESSING:

1 tablespoon dried oregano

1 teaspoon salt

1 teaspoon freshly ground black pepper

3 tablespoons Fischer & Wieser Pomegranate & Mango Chipotle Sauce

1 cup mayonnaise

2 tablespoons minced cilantro

If you're looking for a great way to use up left-over chicken or turkey, try this unusual salad. Your taste buds with thank you, especially for the light, deliciously different tropical fruit tastes.

In a large bowl, mix chopped chicken, onion, celery, bell peppers, corn and nuts. In a separate bowl, whisk together dressing ingredients, blending well. Fold dressing into the chicken & vegetable mixture. Refrigerate until ready to use. Serves 4–6

GRILLED *steak* SALAD

1 peeled cucumber

1 cored, seeded red bell pepper

1 small zucchini

1½ pounds trimmed, boneless, 1 inch thick sirloin steak

½ cup The Original Roasted Raspberry Chipotle Vinaigrette

1 small bunch fresh cilantro, chopped

When time is short and you're thinking healthy, try this fantastic salad. Then again, no one in Texas ever turns down a salad that brings its own steak to the party.

Slice vegetables into matchsticks, about 2 inches long and ¼ inch wide; set aside. Brush steak with 1–2 tablespoons The Original Roasted Raspberry Chipotle Vinaigrette; grill over medium heat 3–4 minutes each side for medium rare. Toss vegetables with 5–6 tablespoons The Original Roasted Raspberry Chipotle Vinaigrette; arrange evenly on four plates. Thinly slice hot steak; arrange over vegetables. Drizzle with additional The Original Roasted Raspberry Chipotle Vinaigrette to taste; sprinkle with cilantro for garnish. Serves 4.

PAULO'S SALAD *from* Messina HOF WINERY*

½ clove garlic

3 anchovies

1 tablespoon minced garlic

2 tablespoons Messina Hof Port

2 tablespoons soy sauce

2 tablespoons Dijon mustard

2 tablespoons olive oil

2 tablespoons balsamic vinegar

2 tablespoons lemon juice

1 egg

12 whole romaine leaves

¼ cup croutons

2 tablespoons grated Romano cheese

When winemaker Paul Bonarrigo's grandfather came to America from Sicily, he brought his recipe for a salad that became famous as a wedding proposal salad. We think of this salad every time we visit Paul and his wife Merrill at Messina Hof, whether the original winery in Bryan or the lovely new satellite in Fredericksburg.

At tableside, rub the bowl with ½ clove of garlic and mash the anchovies into a paste in the bowl. Combine the anchovies, garlic, wine, soy sauce, mustard, oil, vinegar, lemon juice and egg in a bowl; mix well. Add romaine and toss. Top with croutons and Romano cheese. Intended to be eaten with fingers instead of a fork. Serves 2.

* 9996 U.S. Highway 290
830.990.4653
www.messinahof.com

PAPAYA LIME *serrano* *tropical* FRUIT SALAD

1 cup pineapple, cubed

1 cup cantaloupe, cubed

1 cup honeydew melon, cubed

1 cup red seedless grapes

1 cup apple, sliced and cubed

¾ cup Fischer & Wieser Papaya Lime Serrano Sauce

¼ cup chardonnay

Want a light, delicious fruit salad with a hint of zing for your next cookout? Try this delightful salad and just gather in the compliments.

Combine all fruits in large bowl. Blend Fischer & Wieser Papaya Lime Serrano Sauce and chardonnay. Drizzle over fruits; toss lightly. Transfer to cut glass bowl. Serves 8–12.

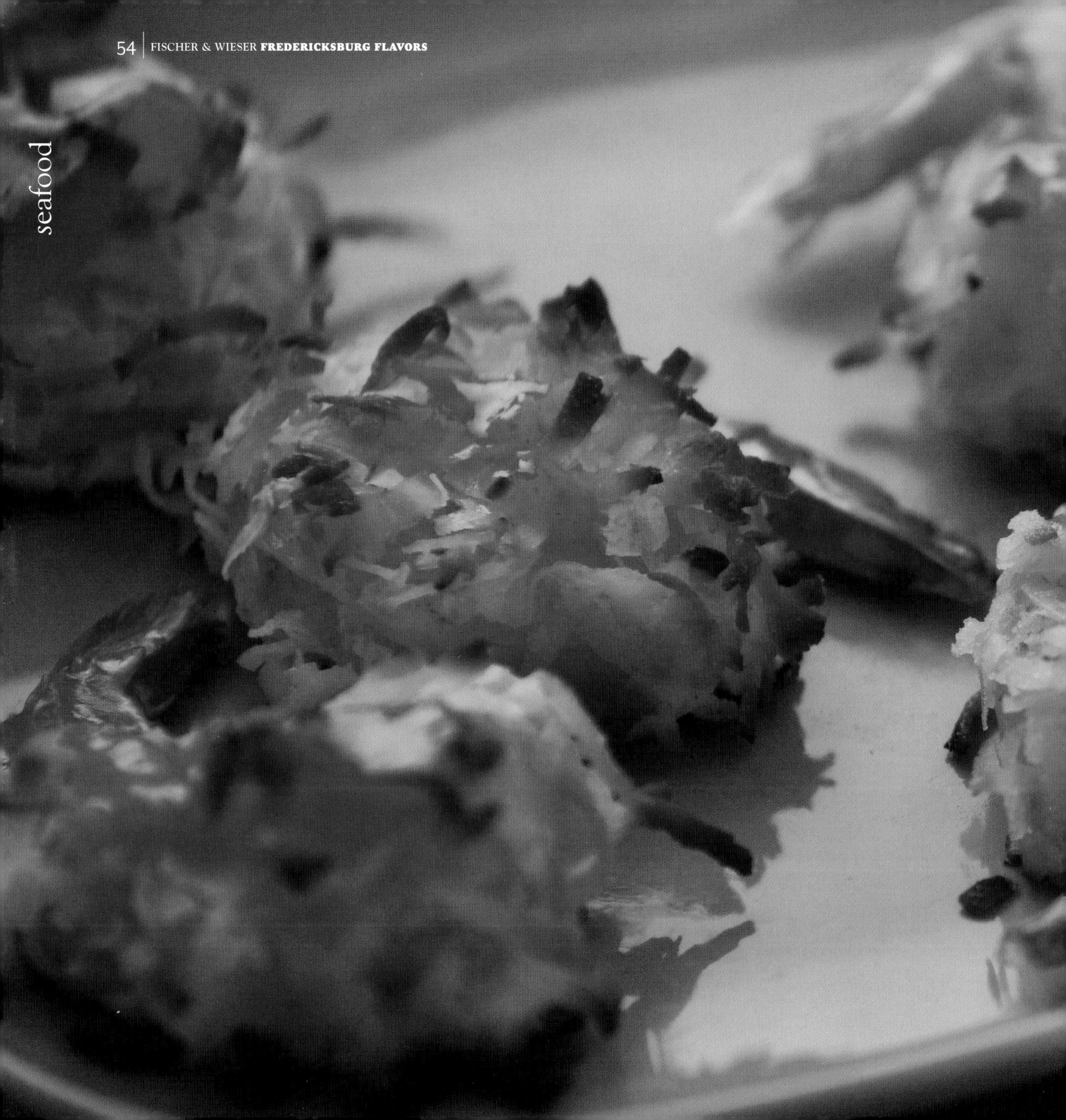

RECIPES

seafood

seafood

SHRIMP *pasta* SALAD

1 cup Fischer & Wieser Cilantro Pepito Pesto Appetizer-Spread

1 cup real mayonnaise

½ teaspoon salt

¼ teaspoon freshly ground black pepper

2 cups raw tubular pasta, such as penne, cooked al dente and drained

2 pounds chilled, small boiled shrimp, roughly chopped

1 (6 ounce) jar marinated artichoke hearts, drained and roughly chopped

6 green onions, chopped, including green tops

Here's a quick and delicious pasta salad for luncheons or dinners. Pair with a green salad and a nice, dry white wine.

Combine the Fischer & Wieser Cilantro Pepito Pesto Appetizer-Spread, mayonnaise, salt and pepper in a bowl; whisk to blend well; set aside. In a larger bowl combine the cooked pasta, boiled shrimp, artichoke hearts and green onions, tossing to blend well. Fold dressing into pasta salad, combining thoroughly. Refrigerate until ready to serve. Serves 4–6.

BAKED COCONUT *shrimp* *with* MILD GREEN *or* RED HOT JALAPEÑO *jelly*

Non-stick cooking spray

24 medium shrimp, peeled and deveined

½ tablespoon garlic and herb seasoning

¼ tablespoon black pepper

1 egg, well beaten

¾ cup flour

¼ cup shredded coconut

1 jar Fischer & Wieser Mild Green or Red Hot Jalapeño Jelly

Try this great recipe as an appetizer, or entree for your next get-together! Baking the shrimp takes the hassle out of the preparations, giving you more time to enjoy your guests.

Preheat oven to 425° F. Coat large baking sheet with non-stick cooking spray. Sprinkle shrimp with garlic and herb seasoning blend and pepper. Place egg, flour, and coconut in small separate bowls. Dip shrimp first in egg, then in flour, and then back in egg, then liberally in coconut. Place shrimp on baking sheet. Bake until golden and crisp for at least 15 minutes. While shrimp is baking, heat Fischer & Wieser Mild Green or Red Hot Jalapeño Jelly in small saucepan; bring to a simmer; cover and keep warm until ready to serve. Serve shrimp with warmed Fischer & Wieser Mild Green or Red Hot Jalapeño Jelly as a dipping sauce. Serves 6.

seafood

BEJAS *grill** SHRIMP ENCHILADAS

WHITE SAUCE:
6 cups heavy cream
4 cups shredded Monterey Jack cheese
4 tablespoons burgundy wine
4 tablespoons corn starch
2 cups shrimp, peeled and butterflied
1–2 teaspoons Old Bay seasoning
1–2 teaspoons fresh dill

MANGO SALSA:
1 cup mango, diced
1 cup red bell pepper, diced
juice of 2–3 lime wedges

8 corn tortillas, dipped in oil

2 cups Mexican rice
2 cups black beans

---

* 209 East Main Street
830.997.5226
www.bejasgrill.com

We've always loved this outpost of creative Southwestern flavors at the heart of Fredericksburg. In particular, we relish the choice between the vibrantly colored dining room and, on the best days of spring and fall, the patio outside. These shrimp enchiladas in a creamy cheese sauce have become a Bejas Grill signature.

Preheat oven to 400° F. In a large pot, heat the heavy cream until it boils. Add the cheese and stir until blended, then add the wine and corn starch. Peel the shrimp and butterfly. Marinate for about 30 minutes using Old Bay seasoning and dill. After the shrimp have marinated, lightly grill approximately 2 minutes, turning once or twice. Rough-chop the shrimp.

To make the quick mango salsa, dice equal parts of mango and red bell pepper. Squeeze the lime juice over the top.

Moisten the tortillas with a little oil and preheat for 30 seconds on the grill, for greater flexibility in rolling. Lay out tortillas, add shrimp and roll gently. Place in a ceramic baking dish, folded side down. Upon completion of all enchiladas, pour cream sauce on top and bake for approximately 10 minutes, until hot and bubbly. Plate enchiladas with rice and beans, and add a couple of spoons of mango salsa on top of each enchilada. Serves 4.

COCONUT SHRIMP *with* HATCH *chile & pineapple* SALSA

28 large shrimp (about 1½ pounds)

⅓ cup cornstarch

¾ teaspoon salt

½–¾ teaspoon ground red pepper

3 large egg whites

1½ cups flaked sweetened coconut

Cooking spray

½–¾ cup Fischer & Wieser Hatch Chile & Pineapple Salsa

We tested this variation that melded Louisiana cooking with Asian flavors in our test kitchen, and our employees loved it! Your friends and family will too.

Preheat oven to 400° F. To prepare shrimp, peel and devein shrimp, leaving tails intact. Rinse shrimp in cold water; drain on paper towels until dry. Combine cornstarch, salt, and red pepper in a shallow dish; stir with a whisk. Place the egg whites in a medium bowl, and beat with a mixer at medium-high speed until frothy (about 2 minutes). Place coconut in a shallow dish. Working with one shrimp at a time, dredge in cornstarch mixture. Dip in egg white; dredge in coconut, pressing gently with fingers. Place shrimp on a baking sheet coated with cooking spray. Repeat the procedure with remaining shrimp, cornstarch mixture, egg white, and coconut. Lightly coat shrimp with cooking spray. Bake at 400° F for 20 minutes or until shrimp are done, turning after 10 minutes. Serve on plate with Fischer & Wieser Hatch Chile & Pineapple Salsa on the side. Spoon over each shrimp and enjoy! Serves 8–12.

seafood

GRILLED *bacon* WRAPPED *shrimp with* MANGO GINGER HABANERO *sauce*

24 large raw shrimp

24 strips of thinly sliced bacon

1 large fresh lime

1¾ cups Fischer & Wieser Mango Ginger Habanero Sauce

Fresh cilantro, finely chopped

These fabulous skewers make the perfect appetizer for parties, and family barbecues. The flavor combination is so good you'll have guests asking for more sauce for dipping.

Shell and devein shrimp leaving tails on. Wrap each shrimp tightly with one strip of bacon. Thread 6 shrimp on each skewer so that they lay flat on their sides on the grill. Grill on medium-high heat for 3–4 minutes per side until bacon is cooked and shrimp are pink. Spritz with half the lime while on the grill. Remove shrimp to serving platter and spritz with remaining lime. Brush with Fischer & Wieser Mango Ginger Habanero Sauce. Sprinkle with chopped cilantro to garnish. Serves 4.

seafood

SWEET, SOUR & *smokey grilled* *shrimp* REMOULADE

2 pounds jumbo shrimp, peeled

¼ cup vegetable oil

2 tablespoons freshly squeezed lemon juice

3 cloves garlic, chopped

1 teaspoon salt

Romaine lettuce leaves

REMOULADE:

¼ cup Fischer & Wieser Sweet, Sour & Smokey Mustard Sauce

¾ cup olive oil

1 tablespoon paprika

½ cup diced celery

1 cup diced green onions

1 teaspoon minced garlic

½ cup finely chopped parsley

1 tablespoon freshly grated horseradish

⅛ teaspoon ground red pepper

2 tablespoons lemon juice

Salt and black pepper to taste

It's nice to remember some days that Texas is just across the Sabine River from Louisiana, with a lot of families (and recipes) moving back and forth over the years. We think this New Orleans classic got better when it swam across the river in our direction.

Place the shrimp in a glass bowl with the oil, lemon juice, garlic and salt, mixing to coat thoroughly. Cover and set the bowl in the refrigerator to marinate for 3 hours. Prepare the remoulade by pouring the mustard sauce into a bowl and gradually adding the olive oil, whisking constantly, followed by all remaining remoulade ingredients. When ready to serve, grill the shrimp over hot coals for 5–7 minutes, turning halfway through. Set shrimp on plates atop lettuce leaves and spoon remoulade over the top and sides. Serves 8.

FIERY *smokehouse* SHRIMP *skewers with* SWEET HEAT MARMALADE *sauce*

48 large raw shrimp, peeled and deveined with tails attached

½ cup Fischer & Wieser Smokehouse Bacon & Chipotle Grilling Sauce

2 tablespoons Fischer & Wieser Hot Habanero Salsa

2 tablespoons Fischer & Wieser Sweet Onion & Garlic Marmalade

2 tablespoons canola oil (plus 1 tablespoon for oiling grates)

2 tablespoons apple cider vinegar

8 (12 inch) water soaked wooden skewers

SAUCE:

¾ cup Fischer & Wieser Apricot Orange Marmalade

1 tablespoon Fischer & Wieser Sweet Heat Mustard

1½ teaspoons prepared horseradish

2 teaspoons finely chopped fresh parsley

Here's a terrific grilled shrimp recipe that's both sweet and hot from our good customer Mary Shivers of Ada, OK.

Place shrimp in a large resealable plastic bag. Puree next five ingredients in a food processor or blender. Reserve ¼ cup for basting. Pour remaining marinade over shrimp. Seal, shake and refrigerate for 2–3 hours. Remove shrimp from marinade and discard liquid. Thread 6 shrimp on each skewer, piercing once near the head and once near the tail. Prepare a grill to medium heat, oiling grates. Grill for 3–4 minutes per side or until shrimp are opaque and grill marks appear, turning and basting with reserved marinade twice. While shrimp are grilling, stir all sauce ingredients together in a small bowl. Serve shrimp with sauce for dipping. Serves 8.

seafood

BERRY *good* SHRIMP *tacos*

½ cup butter

1 cup chopped poblano peppers

½ cup chopped onion

2 cups chopped shrimp (peeled and deveined)

8 ounces cream cheese

¾ cup Fischer & Wieser The Original Roasted Raspberry Chipotle Sauce®

1 cup grated Monterey Jack cheese

8–10 red corn tortillas, softened or steamed

8–10 leaves of red leaf lettuce

This winning recipe was submitted by one of our very good customers, Bill Slingerland.

Melt butter in a 12" skillet. Over medium heat, saute peppers and onions in butter until soft. Add shrimp and stir until shrimp turns pink. Add cream cheese and continue stirring until cheese is melted. Add The Original Roasted Raspberry Chipotle Sauce®. Cook over low heat for 10–15 minutes. Remove from heat and stir in the grated cheese. One by one, place steamed tortillas flat on a plate and place a lettuce leaf on top of each. Spoon about ¼ cup of the shrimp mixture in the center of each lettuce leaf. Fold each tortilla in half like a taco. Serve with Caribbean rice and black beans. Makes 8–10 tacos.

BACON WRAPPED *shrimp* with HIBISCUS & ANCHO CHILE *grilling sauce*

20 large shrimp, raw, deveined & peeled

¾–1 cup Fischer & Wieser Hibiscus & Ancho Chile Grilling Sauce

10 slices bacon, cut in half

½ teaspoon salt

¼ teaspoon pepper

20 toothpicks soaked in water at least 15 minutes

Nothing could be easier, whether you need an appetizer or entree! Great for outdoor barbecues, tail-gate parties, holiday entertaining.

Preheat oven to broil, or a grill to medium-high. Wash and pat shrimp dry. Place in shallow bowl; cover with Fischer & Wieser Hibiscus & Ancho Chile Grilling Sauce and stir to coat. Sprinkle with salt and pepper. Wrap each with a bacon strip and secure with soaked toothpicks. If broiling, place on cookie sheet, place under broiler 5 minutes; turn, broil another 5 minutes until bacon is crispy and done. If grilling, place on grill and turn after 5 minutes; grill until bacon is crispy and done. Serve with additional Fischer & Wieser Hibiscus & Ancho Chile Grilling Sauce. Serves 10–12 as appetizers, or 4 as entree.

SHRIMP *and* CHICKEN *meal* ON A STICK

1 chicken breast, trimmed and cubed

6 jumbo shrimp, peeled and deveined

1 1 pound sirloin steak for grilling, trimmed and cubed

1 zucchini, sliced

1 yellow squash, sliced

1 cup fresh mushrooms, sliced

1 red bell pepper, sliced and cut into squares

1 green bell pepper, sliced and cut into squares

1 onion, cut into wedges and separated

1¾ cups The Original Roasted Raspberry Chipotle Vinaigrette

Fajita seasoning, to taste

1 bunch cilantro

Want a fun and fantastic meal that you can involve your guests and/or family in the preparation? Not only does this fill that bill bigtime, but it's scrumptious in the bargain!

Prepare grill for cooking. Marinate all ingredients in The Original Roasted Raspberry Chipotle Vinaigrette 15–30 minutes. Thread chicken, shrimp, steak zucchini, squash, mushrooms, bell peppers, and onions, alternating all, onto skewers. Sprinkle with fajita seasoning. Grill 15–20 minutes, turning frequently, until juices in meats and shrimp run clear. To serve, remove from skewers to a bed of cilantro and serve with more The Original Roasted Raspberry Chipotle Vinaigrette. Serves 6.

GRILLED *orange* ROUGHY *with* *papaya lime* SERRANO SAUCE

4 orange roughy filets

1¾ cups Fischer & Wieser Papaya Lime Serrano Sauce

1 tablespoon extra virgin olive oil

1 teaspoon cracked black pepper

1 teaspoon sea salt

Orange roughy has become extremely popular across America for its mild, slightly sweet taste—something that makes it a perfect canvas for painting with flavors such as these.

Light charcoal; let burn to a point where the heat allows you to place hand 4" away from grill. Brush the filets with olive oil, season with salt and pepper, and then place on grill, cooking approximately 2 minutes for each side. Pour a generous amount of the Fischer & Wieser Papaya Lime Serrano Sauce over the filets after turning, allowing the sauce to slightly glaze. Serves 4.

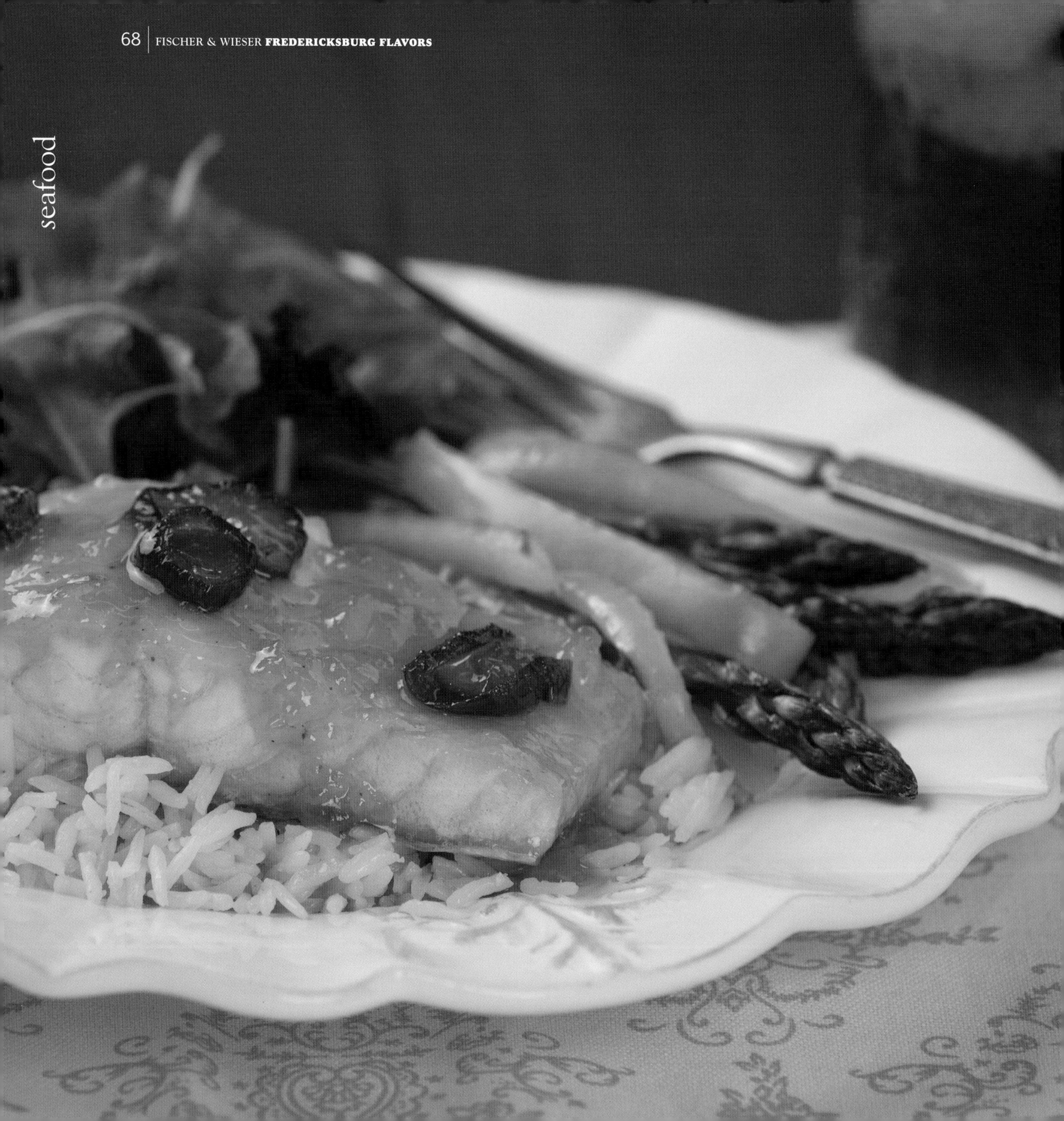

RICH *peach-glazed* SALMON

4 salmon steaks, 6 ounces each

½ cup Fischer & Wieser Jalapeño Peach Preserves

1 teaspoon light soy sauce

¼ teaspoon paprika or cayenne pepper

¼ teaspoon ground ginger

2 large colored bell peppers, seeded, thinly sliced into strips

1 medium yellow onion, thinly sliced into strips

1 tablespoon light olive oil

Kosher salt and freshly ground black pepper

This recipe comes to us from "The Chile Doctor," (www.ChileUnderground.com), who has generously shared it and given us permission to use it. His kind words: "This recipe uses your outstanding Fischer & Wieser Jalapeño Peach Preserves, and it really makes the salmon taste great (in my opinion). I'm not a fan of salmon, but this had me cleaning my plate and wishing it was polite to lick it...If you're a fan of salmon, then you know its rich taste can stand up to stronger flavors in the sauce than, say, trout. Here's a zesty treat for you then!"

Prepare broiler or grill for medium-high, direct heat. Place salmon on nonstick foil or non-stick spray coated broiler sheet. Blend Fischer & Wieser Jalapeño Peach Preserves, soy, paprika or cayenne, and ginger in a small bowl, then brush liberally on fish. Place vegetable strips around fish, spreading out so they'll cook well; brush veggies with oil and then season. Grill fish about 5 inches from heat for 10–12 minutes, or until it begins to flake with a fork. About half-way through, turn the veggies over and brush the fish again with more glaze. Serve with tossed salad, rice and a nice *Liebfraumilch* for a complete and healthy meal.

Got some other vegetable you prefer over peppers and onions? Go right ahead! Just be sure not to use something that takes longer than 10–15 minutes to cook; like say, baked potatoes. Fix them separately. Serves 4.

poultry

RECIPES

poultry

CHICKEN *quesadillas* *with* FISCHER & WIESER *chipotle & corn* SALSA

12 white corn tortillas

5 grilled or baked chicken breasts, sliced into thin slices

1 pound shredded quesadilla or Monterey Jack cheese

2 cups Fischer & Wieser Chipotle & Corn Salsa

Canola oil

Pair these great quesadillas with a side of guacamole on shredded lettuce and you've got yourself a great light meal.

Lay the corn tortillas on a baking sheet. Arrange some of the chicken slices on half of each tortilla. Scatter ⅓ cup of the shredded cheese over the chicken on each tortilla. Spoon some of the Fischer & Wieser Chipotle & Corn Salsa over the cheese. Fold the top of the tortillas over the filling. Heat a thin glaze of canola oil in a large skillet or flat griddle-grill. When oil is medium hot, cook the quesadillas until the cheese has melted and tortillas are slightly browned, turning once with a wide metal spatula. Smash the top of the tortilla to flatten slightly when turned. To serve, cut each quesadilla into two wedges. Arrange on a platter and serve hot with more Fischer & Wieser Chipotle & Corn Salsa on the side. Serves 6.

SMOKEY MESQUITE *mustard & apricot orange* MARMALADE GRILLED *chicken*

½ cup Fischer & Wieser Smokey Mesquite Mustard

¼ cup Fischer & Wieser Apricot Orange Marmalade

2 garlic cloves, minced

4 small boneless skinless chicken breast halves

The unusual combination of flavors in this recipe—the smokiness of the mustard zinging around with the sweet-tangy accents of the marmalade—will leave you wanting more.

Whisk together the Fischer & Wieser Smokey Mesquite Mustard, Fischer & Wieser Apricot Orange Marmalade, and garlic. Place the chicken in a plastic resealable bag. Add ¼ cup of the mustard-marmalade-garlic mixture and turn breasts to coat well. Reserve remaining mixture for sauce. Prepare grill for cooking. Remove chicken from marinade; discard marinade. When fire is medium hot, place chicken breast on oiled rack over fire. Grill 5–6 minutes on each side or until cooked through. Heat remaining mustard-marmalade-garlic mixture in a small saucepan over low heat. Serve chicken with sauce. Serves 4.

CHICKEN *marsala* *from* WEST END *pizza**

½ cup all-purpose flour

Salt

Black pepper

4 (6–8 ounce) boneless, skinless chicken breasts, cut in halves and pounded thin

2 tablespoons olive oil

8 tablespoons butter

6 cups sliced mushrooms

1½ cup Marsala wine

1½ cup chicken broth

Chopped chives, for garnish

---

* 232 West Main Street
830.990.8646
www.westendpizzacompany.com

Our friends at West End Pizza make a great version of their namesake product. But we also love their version of the Italian classic. Serve it with your favorite pasta.

In a shallow bowl or plate combine the flour, a pinch of salt and pepper and stir to combine thoroughly. Quickly dredge the chicken breast halves in the seasoned flour mixture, shaking to remove any excess flour. Heat the oil in a large skillet over medium-high heat until very hot but not smoking. Add 3 tablespoons of the butter and cook the chicken breasts until golden brown on both sides, about 2–3 minutes per side. Do this in batches if the pieces don't fit comfortably in the pan. Transfer to a plate.

Add 2 tablespoons of the remaining butter to the pan and add the mushrooms. Cook, stirring frequently, until mushrooms are golden brown around the edges and have given off their liquid. Add the Marsala wine and bring to a boil, scraping to remove any browned bits from the bottom of the pan. When the wine has reduced by half, add the chicken broth and cook for 3 minutes, or until the sauce has thickened slightly. Lower the heat to medium and return the chicken breasts to the pan and continue to cook until they are cooked through and the sauce has thickened, about 5 to 6 minutes. Swirl in the remaining butter, add salt and pepper to taste. Garnish with chopped chives and serve immediately with pasta. Serves 4.

poultry

TURKEY *quesadillas with* FISCHER & WIESER *artichoke* *& olive* SALSA

12 white corn tortillas

1½ cups chopped turkey breast, sliced into thin slices

1 pound shredded quesadilla cheese, or substitute Monterey Jack

2 cups Fischer & Wieser Artichoke & Olive Salsa

Canola oil

Quesadillas with artichokes and olives flavoring them are a little unusual—but great! Add guacamole on shredded lettuce to make the tastes really pop. And of course, this is great with leftover Thanksgiving turkey.

Lay the corn tortillas on a baking sheet. Arrange some of the chicken slices on half of each tortilla. Scatter ⅓ cup of the shredded cheese over the chicken on each tortilla. Spoon some of the Fischer & Wieser Artichoke & Olive Salsa over the cheese. Fold the top of the tortillas over the filling. Heat a thin glaze of canola oil in a large skillet or flat griddle-grill. When oil is medium hot, cook the quesadillas until the cheese has melted and tortillas are slightly browned, turning once with a wide metal spatula. Smash the top of the tortilla to flatten slightly when turned. To serve, cut each quesadilla into two wedges. Arrange on a platter and serve hot with more Fischer & Wieser Artichoke & Olive Salsa on the side. Serves 6.

ARTICHOKE *and olive* *arroz* CON POLLO

2 tablespoons extra-virgin olive oil

4 boneless, skinless chicken breast halves, cut into bite-sized pieces

1 small onion, chopped

1 red sweet pepper, chopped

1 teaspoon minced garlic

½ teaspoon garlic powder

½ teaspoon onion powder

Salt and freshly ground black pepper

Crushed red pepper to taste

1 (10 ounce) package yellow rice mix

Water

½ cup Fischer & Wieser Artichoke and Olive Salsa

⅔ cup frozen green peas

Arroz con Pollo, sometimes referred to as Chicken with Yellow Rice and a less extravagant version of the paella from Valencia, is one of those Old World Spanish dishes that found a lasting home in the New World, especially in Cuba. Both colonizer and colony should happily claim the recipe once we've added our delightfully unusual salsa.

Heat the olive oil in a large pot or paella-style pan with a lid. Add the chicken pieces and cook until golden brown, then add the onion, red pepper and garlic, stirring till they start to soften. Season with garlic and onion powders, salt, pepper and crushed red pepper. Pour in the rice mix and stir for a minute or two, till grains are coated with oil. Add the amount of water called for in package directions, then stir in the artichoke and olive salsa. Add the frozen peas, stir to combine and bring to a boil. Cover the pot, reduce heat to medium-low and cook until liquid is absorbed and rice is done, about 20 minutes. Serves 6–8.

poultry

LAVENDER *chicken breasts* *from* BECKER VINEYARDS*

6 boneless, skinless chicken breasts

½ cup lemon juice

1 teaspoon dried thyme

1 teaspoon dried culinary lavender, finely ground

Salt

Black pepper

2 tablespoons extra-virgin olive oil

5 tablespoons unsalted butter, softened

2 cups thinly sliced mushrooms

⅓ cup minced shallot

¾ cup champagne or other sparkling wine

¾ cup chicken broth

1 teaspoon all-purpose flour

2 tablespoons chopped fresh parsley

Fresh lavender sprigs for garnish

* 464 Becker Farms Road, Stonewall
830.644.2128
www.beckervineyards.com

As though making some of the best wine in Texas weren't impressive enough, our friends Dr. Richard Becker and his wife Bunny have launched a successful lavender-growing operation that makes their whole place down the road in Stonewall look like the South of France. They even have an annual Lavender Festival at Becker Vineyards, with chefs exploring culinary uses like this.

Sprinkle the chicken on both sides with lemon juice, thyme and lavender, then let marinate for 30 minutes. Lightly season with salt and pepper. Heat the oil and 4 tablespoons of butter in a skillet and brown the chicken breasts on both sides. Remove from the skillet. Add the mushroom and shallot, stirring about 5 minutes, followed by the champagne, and broth. Simmer for 10 minutes.

Mix the flour and remaining butter in a small bowl and whisk the mixture into the skillet, until the sauce thickens. Return the chicken and simmer for 14 minutes, until cooked through. Add the parsley. Serve hot garnished with lavender sprigs. Serves 6.

GRILLED WHOLE *chicken basted in* MILD GREEN *or* RED HOT JALAPEÑO *jelly*

3 tablespoons butter

¼–½ cup chicken broth

1¾ cup Fischer & Wieser Mild Green or Red Hot Jalapeño Jelly

1 (3 pound) roasting chicken

The choice is yours when it comes to our pepper jelly: we have a mild one and a hot one, and a lot of days around the test kitchen our employees can't decide which they like better.

Melt butter in saucepan. Add ¼ cup chicken broth and Fischer & Wieser Mild Green or Red Hot Jalapeño Jelly. Blend together and bring to a boil over medium heat; simmer until broth cooks down and creates a glaze, adding more broth if needed. Cook chicken on slow pit for about 2 hours until golden brown, basting with Fischer & Wieser Mild Green or Red Hot Jalapeño Jelly glaze every 15 minutes. Serves 6–8.

Also try the glaze above over grilled shrimp, pork, or lamb.

PEACH SALSA *chicken* FIESTA

¼ cup canola oil

¼ cup onion, diced

1 pound chicken, cubed

2 cups Fischer & Wieser Das Peach Haus® Peach Salsa

1¾ cups canned corn, drained

1¾ cups canned black beans, drained and rinsed

Sweet and spicy peach salsa added to your favorite meat, corn and black beans—what a great way to use up leftover chicken, pork or beef stew meat!

Brown onion in oil until tender; add meat and brown. Stir in Fischer & Wieser Das Peach Haus® Peach Salsa, corn, and black beans. Simmer 20–25 minutes. Serve with white or Spanish rice. Serves 4.

SPICY SESAME *stir fry* CHICKEN

3 tablespoons oil

2 whole boneless, skinless chicken breasts, ⅜" julienned

2 stalks celery, sliced diagonally

1 red bell pepper, julienned

1 cup assorted mushrooms

1 can water chestnuts, sliced

3 green onions, sliced diagonally

1 baby bok choy, chopped in large pieces

¾ cup Fischer & Wieser Spicy Sesame Stir Fry & Dipping Sauce

2 tablespoons black sesame seeds

Stir fry is just naturally quick and delicious, one of the niftiest additions in decades to the American cook's bag of culinary tricks. This one is also tantalizing.

Brown chicken in oil. Remove from pan. Add vegetables and stir-fry for 2–3 minutes. Return chicken to pan and heat through. Add Fischer & Wieser Spicy Sesame Stir Fry & Dipping Sauce and black sesame seeds. Serve over rice. Serves 2.

SPICY SESAME STIR FRY CHICKEN

CHICKEN *with* WHOLE *lemon &* FIG SAUCE

1¼ cup Fischer & Wieser Whole Lemon
& Fig Marmalade

¼ cup water

½ pound dried figs

10 lemon slices

4 boneless, skinless chicken breasts

Fajita seasoning or lemon pepper to taste

1 teaspoon dried parsley

1 tablespoon chopped fresh parsley

Fischer & Wieser Whole Lemon & Fig
Marmalade used in this recipe makes a luscious
sauce unlike anything you've ever tasted before.

Preheat oven to 350° F. In a small bowl, combine Fischer & Wieser
Whole Lemon & Fig Marmalade and water; set aside. Place figs and
6 lemon slices in the bottom of a baking dish which has been sprayed
with non-stick cooking spray. Arrange chicken breasts on top, then
pour Fischer & Wieser Whole Lemon & Fig Marmalade and water
mixture on top. Sprinkle with fajita seasoning or lemon pepper and
dried parsley to taste. Bake for 35 minutes, basting frequently (turn
figs if they begin to brown). With a slotted spoon, remove chicken,
figs and lemon slices from baking dish and place on warm platter.
Skim fat from cooking juices, then pour over chicken as sauce.
Garnish with fresh parsley and remaining 4 lemon slices. Serves 4.

ASPARAGUS *and chicken* manicotti **WITH MOM'S** *garlic* **& BASIL** *spaghetti sauce*

1 box (14) tubular (manicotti, cannelloni) pasta

2½ cups ricotta cheese

2 cups shredded mozzarella cheese

¾ cup Italian seasoned bread crumbs

½ teaspoon salt

½ teaspoon minced garlic

¼–½ teaspoon garlic salt, as desired

½ cup chopped parsley

6 cups Mom's Garlic & Basil Spaghetti Sauce

1 bunch fresh baby asparagus

4 fully cooked Parmesan or Italian Seasoned Chicken Breasts

Simple and quick to prepare, this one-dish meal will turn you into a gourmet chef before you know it. Serve with a green salad and Italian bread sticks to complete the menu.

Carefully place pasta tubes a few at a time into 6–8 quarts of rapidly boiling salted water. Cook 8–10 minutes, stirring occasionally. Do not overcook. Drain. Allow to cool slightly. Combine Ricotta and shredded Mozarella cheeses, Italian bread crumbs, salt, minced garlic, garlic salt and chopped parsley. Pour half the Mom's Garlic & Basil Spaghetti Sauce in 13" x 9" x 2" rectangular baking dish. Stuff the cooked pasta with filling.

Arrange stuffed pasta tubes on sauce. Steam asparagus 3–5 minutes in vegetable steamer. Thaw and warm fully cooked Parmesan or Italian Seasoned Chicken Breasts in microwave, 3–4 minutes. Dice chicken breasts. Place steamed asparagus and diced chicken breasts over stuffed pasta tubes. Pour remaining Mom's Garlic & Basil Spaghetti Sauce over all. Sprinkle with additional mozzarella cheese the last 10 minutes of baking. Bake in 350° F oven approximately 30 minutes. Serves 8–12.

poultry

ARTICHOKE *and asiago* CHEESE *pasta chicken* & SHRIMP

1 (10 ounce) package penne pasta

1 bunch fresh asparagas, each stalk cut into 2" strips

2 tablespoons butter

1 small package Tyson chicken strips

2 cups small deveined shrimp

3½ cups Mom's Artichoke & Asiago Cheese Pasta Sauce

Anyone who's ever sampled a molten casserole at a potluck dinner or party knows the joys of artichoke and cheese occupying the same space. This recipe takes that casserole and makes it a satisfying pasta entree.

Prepare penne pasta according to package directions; drain. Steam asparagas until fork-tender. Add to pasta. Saute chicken strips and shrimp in butter. Add chicken and shrimp to pasta and asparagas. Pour Mom's Artichoke and Asiago Cheese Sauce over mixture; mix well. Serve hot with breadsticks and a green salad. Serves 4–6.

SWEET & *spicy* CHICKEN

¼ cup Fischer & Wieser Apricot Orange Marmalade

¼ cup Fischer & Wieser Spicy Garlic Steak & Grilling Sauce

1 teaspoon salt

1 tablespoon cilantro

2 chicken breasts

Sweet and spicy is a big deal in Hawaii, as we see in this tasty chicken recipe from good customer Lynne Akiko of Honolulu.

Mix Fischer & Wieser Apricot Orange Marmalade and Fischer & Wieser Spicy Garlic Steak & Grilling Sauce, salt, and cilantro in a mixing bowl. Marinate chicken breast in sauce for about an hour. Heat grill to medium. Grill chicken breasts until juices run clear, approximately 10 minutes per side, depending on thickness of chicken breasts. Serves 2.

MAPLE *chipotle* SWEET *potato* MASH

3 pounds sweet potatoes, peeled and cubed

⅔ stick butter

¼ cup maple syrup

1 tablespoon canned chipotles in adobo, minced

Kosher salt

White pepper

Boil sweet potatoes in enough water to cover until tender (about 20–30 minutes) and drain from water completely. Place drained sweet potatoes in a medium size bowl and mash with butter, syrup and canned chipotles in adobo while still hot. Adjust seasoning with salt and white pepper. Serves 6.

poultry

BACON *wrapped* JALAPEÑO *stuffed* LOCKHART QUAIL *from* CABERNET *Grill**

JALAPEÑO STUFFED QUAIL:

12 semi-boneless Lockhart quail

6 fresh jalapeños, cut in half lengthwise

12 strips applewood smoked bacon

Kosher salt

Freshly ground black pepper

2 cups rosemary-raspberry demi-glace, warm (see recipe)

Rosemary sprigs

ROSEMARY-RASPBERRY DEMI-GLACE:

2 tablespoon butter or vegetable oil

2 small shallots, minced

2 teaspoon fresh rosemary, minced

1 cup veal demi-glace

1 cup The Original Roasted Raspberry Chipotle Sauce®

Kosher salt

Freshly ground black pepper

* 2805 South Hwy 16
830.990.5734
www.cabernetgrill.com

We're always happy when one of our great Fredericksburg chefs chooses to showcase our Fischer & Wieser products on their menu, proving again how far these flavors can travel when a chef cooks with skill and creativity. The kudos here go to executive chef Ross Burtwell of Cabernet Grill.

Stuff each quail with a jalapeño half and wrap with one slice of bacon. Secure bacon to the bird with a toothpick. Prepare a grill with mesquite wood and bring to a medium high heat. Season quail accordingly with salt and pepper. Lightly oil the cooking grate on the grill and add quail. Cook for about 5 minutes on each side, or until the juices from inside the quail run clear and the bacon begins to crisp up a bit. Remove toothpicks from the quail and set on a serving platter. Top with raspberry demi-glace and garnish with rosemary sprigs. Serve hot with Maple Chipotle Sweet Potato Mash (recipe on previous page). Serves 6.

ROSEMARY-RASPBERRY DEMI-GLACE:

Heat a small sauce pan over medium heat and add butter, shallots and rosemary. Cook shallots lightly until they begin to turn translucent. Do not allow them to brown. Stir in demi-glace and The Original Roasted Raspberry Chipotle Sauce® and heat through. Adjust seasoning accordingly with salt and pepper. Serves 6.

pork

RECIPES

pork

pork

GRILLED *pork* TENDERLOIN *with* FISCHER & WIESER *the* ORIGINAL *roasted* RASPBERRY *chipotle* SAUCE®

1 (1 pound) pork tenderloin, trimmed of fat and silverskin

1 teaspoon salt

Freshly ground black pepper to taste

1½ cups Fischer & Wieser The Original Roasted Raspberry Chipotle Sauce®

This is the most delicious and easy-to-prepare way to serve pork tenderloin you are likely to ever try.

Marinate meat in 1 cup Fischer & Wieser The Original Roasted Raspberry Chipotle Sauce® for 1–8 hours. Remove from marinade and season with salt and pepper. Preheat grill to medium heat. Grill to an internal temperature of 145° F, about 25–30 minutes. Baste often with additional Fischer & Wieser The Original Roasted Raspberry Chipotle Sauce®. Remove meat to a cutting board; cover loosely with foil and allow to rest 10 minutes before slicing (½" thick slices). Pour any meat drippings over the meat before serving. Serves 4–6.

pork

MISS JANE'S *mesquite mustard* PORK TENDERLOIN

1 (4–6 pound) pork tenderloin

¼ cup olive oil

¼ cup Fischer & Wieser Smokey Mesquite Mustard

½ teaspoon coarse salt

¼ teaspoon black pepper, freshly ground

Pork tenderloin crusted with our Fischer & Wieser Smokey Mesquite Mustard—what a combination. The basic idea is classic, but the flavors are new and exciting.

Coat pork tenderloin with olive oil. Mix Fischer & Wieser Smokey Mesquite Mustard with coarse salt and freshly ground pepper to taste. Coat the tenderloin with the mustard mixture. Roast in 375° F oven for approximately 30 minutes or until internal temperature reaches 155–160° F. Remove from oven, cover loosely with foil and let sit for 10 minutes. Slice horizontally, serve.

One of the first people to share a recipe using Fischer & Wieser products was our dear friend Jane Woellhoff who with her husband Ron own Showcase Antiques in Fredericksburg. Here are Case and Deanna Fischer and Jane and Ron Woellhoff at the Nimitz Museum grand opening of the new George HW Bush Gallery.

PORK TENDERLOIN *with* *peach-cognac* SAUCE

2 cups Fischer & Wieser Das Peach Haus® Peach Salsa

1 cup chicken broth

¼ cup cognac or other brandy

½ teaspoon Worcestershire sauce

2 pork tenderloins, about 2 pounds

Grilling or Creole seasoning

2 tablespoons olive oil

Pork is one of those meats that always seem to pair well with fruit-based sauces. In particular, Fredericksburg being the heart of Texas peach country, we love what happens when it's cooked with our own peach salsa and a bit of cognac.

To prepare the Peach-Cognac Sauce, combine salsa, chicken broth, cognac and Worcestershire in a saucepan and bring to a boil. Reduce heat to a simmer while preparing the pork. Preheat oven to 350° F. Wash tenderloins and pat dry. Remove excess fat and silver skin. Sprinkle the tenderloins all over with seasoning. Heat olive oil in a large skillet over medium-high heat. Sear the tenderloins on all sides, about 6–8 minutes total. Transfer the tenderloins to a baking pan. Add the peach sauce and cover the pan with foil. Set in the oven for about 20 minutes, or until a meat thermometer registers 145°–150° F in the thickest part. Slice and serve with lots of sauce. Serves 4–6.

pork

BRAISED *pork* SHANKS *from* Fredericksburg HERB FARM*

Kosher salt

Whole black peppercorns

6 pork shanks

6 ounces rendered bacon fat
or canola oil

2 yellow onion, peeled and cut into
1" pieces

1 carrot, peeled and cut into1"pieces

1–2 celery ribs, washed and cut into
1" pieces

4 cloves garlic or more if you love garlic

48 ounces roasted chicken stock
(you may not need all of the stock)

2 bay leaves

2 thyme sprigs

1 cup dry white wine

1–2 ounces cold butter

---

* 405 Whitney Street
830.997.8615
www.fredericksburgherbfarm.com

The Fredericksburg Herb Farm, which grows a fair portion of what they cook in their restaurant called the Farm House Bistro, does a wonderful job of elevating the downhome flavors of Texas till they meet up with great tastes from France and Italy. Here's a wonderful ocean-crossing recipe from executive chef Asa Thornton.

Season shanks thoroughly with the kosher salt. If possible season 24 hours in advance. Heat oven to 275° F. In a heavy bottomed deep frying pan heat half of the rendered bacon fat or canola oil until it is almost smoking. Add 3 of the pork shanks and cook over medium high heat until brown and crusty all over. Transfer the shanks to a pan that is deep enough to accommodate all of the shanks, vegetables and roasted chicken stock. Pour out and discard hot bacon fat (use and old coffee can for this) and brown the remaining 3 pork shanks in the remaining bacon fat. Add the remaining pork shanks to the deep pan with the other shanks.

Pour off most of the fat and add the vegetables and aromatics to the skillet and cook over medium low heat until lightly caramelized. Add the wine, bring to a boil and reduce at a simmer until the pan is almost dry. Add as much chicken stock as the frying pan can hold without boiling over and bring to a simmer; skim any fat that rises to the surface.

Pour the hot stock and vegetables over the pork until the shanks are covered by two thirds of the way. You may need to add some of the cold stock to the braising pan. Cook in oven for 3–4 hours, or until the meat is almost falling off the bone. Turn shanks periodically so that they cook evenly. Remove from oven and let set at room temperature for 45 minutes. Remove shanks and place on a plate. Strain braising jus and place in a pot. Bring to a simmer and skim fat from surface. Reduce jus until the seasoning is to your liking. The more you reduce the more flavorful the jus will be. Reducing also concentrates the salt.

Place shanks back in simmering jus for 10 minutes to reheat. Turn off of heat and finish with a small amount of cold butter if you would like. A potato puree or roasted new potatoes will go well with the shanks. Serves 6.

pork

BABY BACK RIBS *with* FISCHER & WIESER *all purpose* *vegetable & meat* MARINADE

1 (4–5 pound) rack baby back ribs

1½ cups Fischer & Wieser All Purpose Vegetable & Meat Marinade

Mmmm! Here are some tender juicy baby back ribs that melt in your mouth, marinated first in our All Purpose Vegetable & Meat Marinade. Now if we can all just sing that "baby back ribs" jingle. Key of C, please.

Place baby back bibs one layer deep in shallow dish. Pour Fischer & Wieser All Purpose Vegetable & Meat Marinade over and under ribs. Cover; place in refrigerator. Marinate 1–8 hours. Remove from refrigerator and allow ribs to reach room temperature. Prepare barbecue (medium heat). Cut rib racks into 4 to 6 rib sections. Arrange ribs on barbecue. Grill until meat is tender, occasionally turning ribs with tongs, about 40 minutes. Using tongs, transfer ribs to work surface. Cut rib sections between bones into individual ribs. Warm additional Fischer & Wieser All Purpose Vegetable & Meat Marinade to serve alongside ribs. Serves 4–6.

To roast, place ribs, fat side up, on rack above roasting pan in 425° F oven and allow them to sear for 10 minutes. Pour off any grease that accumulates in pan. Lower temperature to 350° F. Baste with additional Fischer & Wieser All Purpose Vegetable & Meat Marinade; roast 20 minutes. Turn ribs over and baste again. Roast an additional 20 minutes. Cut ribs apart and serve. Serves 4–6.

pork

SAUSAGE *wraps with* BRAT HAUS *beer* MUSTARD

Anyone for sausage wraps? You will be when you try them with Fischer & Wieser Brat Haus Beer Mustard slathered on them! Can you say *gemutlickheit?*

---

6 (5–6) inch beef or pork smoked linked sausages, or brats
6 large flour tortillas
⅓–½ cup Fischer & Wieser Brat Haus
Beer Mustard

Preheat gas or char grill. Grill sausages until thoroughly heated, approximately 20 minutes (10 minutes/side). Remove sausages or brats from grill; place on warm pie plate; cover with foil. Place flour tortillas on grill and warm. To serve, place one sausage or brat on each flour tortilla. Slather generously with Fischer & Wieser Brat Haus Beer Mustard. Roll up tortilla and serve. Serves 6.

BAKED HAM *with charred pineapple* BOURBON GLAZE

8–10 pound fully cooked boneless smoked ham

Whole cloves

1¾ cup Fischer & Wieser Charred Pineapple Bourbon Sauce

Baked ham is one of our favorite foods during the holiday season, as well as any time of the year. The rich aroma of the ham in the oven wafting through the house brings back memories of holidays past. Of course, every good baked ham needs an equally good basting sauce, and Fischer & Wieser has you covered. Well, we have the ham covered anyway.

Preheat oven to 325° F. Place ham, fat side up, on a rack in shallow open roasting pan. Bake uncovered for 2½ hours. Remove from oven. Increase oven temperature to 450° F. With sharp knife, make diagonal cuts in the top fat layer of ham, about 1½ inches apart, to form a diamond pattern. Stud the center of each diamond with a whole clove. Pour half the Fischer & Wieser Charred Pineapple Bourbon Sauce over the ham; bake 10 minutes. Pour the remaining sauce over the ham and bake an additional 10 minutes. Allow ham to stand for 20 minutes before slicing. Pass additional Fischer & Wieser Charred Pineapple Bourbon Sauce in a sauce bowl. Serves 14–16.

pork

BAKED HAM *sandwiches* *with harvest* APPLE CIDER *glaze*

8–10 pound fully cooked boneless smoked ham

Whole cloves

1¾ cups Fischer & Wieser Harvest Apple Cider Glaze

Thinly sliced Granny Smith apples

Here's a different flavor spin on baked ham, one that's as all-American as apple pie. And you don't have to wait for dessert to enjoy it.

Preheat oven to 325° F. Place the ham, fat side up, on a wire rack in shallow open roasting pan. With a sharp knife, make diagonal cuts in the top fat layer of the ham, about 1½ inches apart, to form a diamond pattern. Stud the center of each diamond with a whole clove. Pour 1 cup of Fischer & Wieser Harvest Apple Cider Glaze over the ham. Bake, uncovered, for about 2½ hours, basting often with additional glaze. Allow ham to rest for 15 minutes before slicing. Pile slices on sourdough bread and drizzle with additional sauce. Garnish with apple slices. Serves 10–12.

HAM STEAKS *with* FISCHER & WIESER *harvest apple* CIDER GLAZE

For a quick and easy meal, try this tasty entree using our rich-tasting Harvest Apple Cider Glaze poured over a lovely ham steak.

4 tablespoons butter

1 (2 pound) ham steak

1 cup Fischer & Wieser Harvest Apple Cider Glaze

1½ cups chicken stock

Melt the butter in a heavy 12" skillet over medium heat. Add the ham steak and pour the Fischer & Wieser Harvest Apple Cider Glaze over the top. Cook the steak to brown on one side, about 10 minutes. As the sauce begins to thicken add the chicken stock and turn the ham steak over. Stir bottom of pan to release any browned bits of meat glaze. Cook for 10 additional minutes. Slice into individual portions and top with the glaze from the skillet. Serve hot. Serves 2–4.

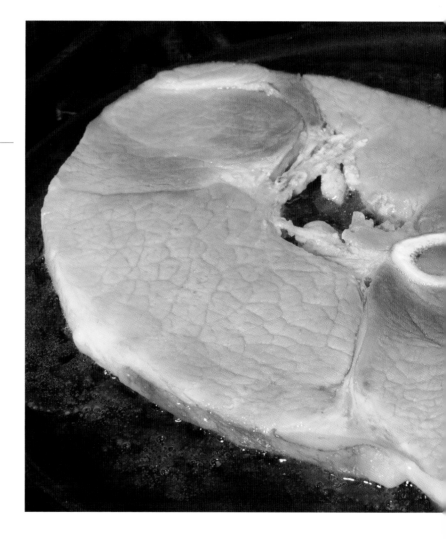

pork

BRANDIED *jalapeño* *peach* PORK CHOPS

4 (1 inch thick) pork loin chops

1 teaspoon salt

½ teaspoon pepper

2 tablespoons vegetable oil

2 tablespoons unsalted butter

½ cup thinly sliced shallots

1 teaspoon finely chopped thyme

¼ cup plus 1 tablespoon brandy, divided

1 (10 ounce) bag frozen peaches, thawed (or fresh in season)

⅓ cup Fischer & Wieser Jalapeño Peach Preserves

If you're looking for a presentation with pizzazz, look no further. Succulent and juicy pork chops with a dramatically prepared brandy-jalapeño peach flambe sauce can't fail to impress your guests. As they say, though, be careful when you're playing with fire.

Rinse chops and pat dry; sprinkle with salt and pepper as desired. Heat oil in a 12 inch heavy skillet over medium heat until it shimmers. Cook pork chops, turning once, until browned and just cooked through, or until meat thermometer inserted in thickest part reads 145° F for 15 seconds, 10–12 minutes total. Transfer to a warm platter, loosely covered with foil. Pour off all but 1 tablespoon fat from skillet. Heat butter in skillet over medium heat until foam dies down. Cook shallots with thyme, stirring occasionally, until tender and golden-brown, about 5 minutes. Add ¼ cup brandy to skillet and carefully ignite with a kitchen match (use caution; flames will shoot up). Cook over medium heat, scraping bottom of skillet to loosen brown bits.

When flames subside, add peaches, Fischer & Wieser Jalapeño Peach Preserves, and ¼ teaspoon each of salt and pepper and simmer, covered, until peaches are tender and juicy, about 3 minutes. Stir in remaining tablespoon brandy, any meat juices from platter, and salt and pepper to taste. Spoon sauce over chops. Serves 4.

FOUR-STAR *black* RASPBERRY *chipotle* GRILLED *pork tenderloin*

2 pork tenderloins, each about 1 pound, trimmed of silverskin

2 tablespoons minced fresh rosemary

2 tablespoons minced fresh sage

3 large garlic cloves, minced

1 teaspoon salt

1 teaspoon freshly ground black pepper

1 cup extra-virgin olive oil

1–1½ cups Fischer & Wieser Four Star Black Raspberry Chipotle Sauce

For a really impressive meal with little muss or fuss, nothing is easier than grilled pork tenderloin. When cooked properly, it's tender and juicy and very, very flavorful. Add Fischer & Wieser Four Star Black Raspberry Chipotle Sauce and you have created a masterpiece.

Preheat char grill to medium. In a small bowl combine rosemary, sage, garlic, salt, black pepper and olive oil. Whisk to blend well. Rub some of the oil mixture over each tenderloin, then grill, turning often, until meat registers 145° F on an instant-read meat thermometer, about 20–30 minutes. Baste often with remaining herb and oil mixture. Remove meat from grill, cover loosely with foil and set aside to rest for 10 minutes before slicing. While meat is resting, heat the Fischer & Wieser Four Star Black Raspberry Chipotle Sauce in a saucepan. Slice the meat on the bias about ½ inch thick. Fan the slices out on each serving plate and spoon a portion of the heated sauce down the middle of the slices. Serve hot. Serves 6.

pork

SLICED HAM *with* HATCH *chile & pineapple* SALSA

1 tablespoon flour

1 browning bag

½–¾ cup Fischer & Wieser Hatch Chile & Pineapple Salsa

1 (1½ pound) sliced center cut ham, ¾–1 inch thick

Nothing could be easier than this quick and delicious way to prepare sliced ham. And the counterpoint of pineapple with the famed New Mexico chile peppers is amazing.

Heat oven to 350° F. Place flour in browning bag, close top, and shake bag. Place approximately ⅓ cup Fischer & Wieser Hatch Chile & Pineapple Salsa in bag and mix with flour. Place ham slice on top of salsa flour mixture. Pour remainder of Fischer & Wieser Hatch Chile & PIneapple Salsa on top of ham slice. Close bag and puncture holes in the bag. Place in oven and bake 20–25 minutes, or until ham slice is completely done, slightly browned around edges. Remove ham slice from bag. Pour juices into bowl. Serve with juices from browning bag on top of ham. Serves 2–4.

GRILLED *pork* TENDERLOIN *with* FISCHER & WIESER *plum* CHIPOTLE *grilling sauce*

1 (1 pound) pork tenderloin, trimmed of fat and silverskin

1 teaspoon salt

freshly ground black pepper to taste

1½ cups Fischer & Wieser Plum Chipotle Grilling Sauce

Here's another great recipe for pork tenderloin, this time cooked on the grill. The charry and lightly smoky taste is a welcome addition.

Marinate meat in 1 cup Fischer & Wieser Plum Chipotle Grilling Sauce for 1–8 hours. Remove from marinade and season with salt and pepper. Preheat grill to medium heat. Grill to an internal temperature of 145° F, about 25–30 minutes. Baste often with additional Fischer & Wieser Plum Chipotle Grilling Sauce. Remove meat to a cutting board; cover loosely with foil and allow to rest 10 minutes before slicing (½" thick slices). Pour any meat drippings over the meat before serving. Serves 4–6.

May substitute Fischer & Wieser The Original Roasted Raspberry Chipotle Sauce® or Fischer & Wieser Pomegranate & Mango Chipotle Sauce

pork

PORK & PLUM *chipotle* STIR *fry*

12 ounces pork tenderloin,
cut into 1 inch cubes

2 tablespoons cornstarch

3 tablespoons peanut oil

4 large garlic cloves, peeled
and smashed

1 large onion, halved, then sliced into ½
inch thick slices

1 large green bell pepper, cut into strips

½ cup slivered bamboo shoots

⅓ cup chicken stock

1¾ cups Fischer & Wieser Plum Chipotle
Grilling Sauce

2 cups cooked white rice

For a fantastic new twist on stir-fry, try this excellent entree. Everybody's tried sweet and sour pork in some Chinese restaurant somewhere. With humility—okay, so this is Texas, so maybe *not so much*—we're here to tell you that this pork stirfry will set the bar for all such dishes pretty dern high.

Toss the pork tenderloin cubes in a bowl with the cornstarch, coating all pieces of the pork well; set aside. Heat the peanut oil in a wok over high heat. When oil is very hot, toss in the smashed garlic cloves and stir fry until they are lightly browned. Remove the garlic with a slotted spoon and discard. Add the pork cubes to the hot oil and stir fry until they are seared on the outside, about 1½ minutes. Remove with slotted spoon and set aside. Add the onion, bell pepper and bamboo shoots to the skillet and stir fry for 2 minutes, or until onion is slightly wilted and transparent. Stir in the chicken stock and Fischer & Wieser Plum Chipotle Grilling Sauce, blending well. Add the pork cubes back to the wok and cook for 2 minutes to finish cooking the pork. Serve over hot rice. Serves 4.

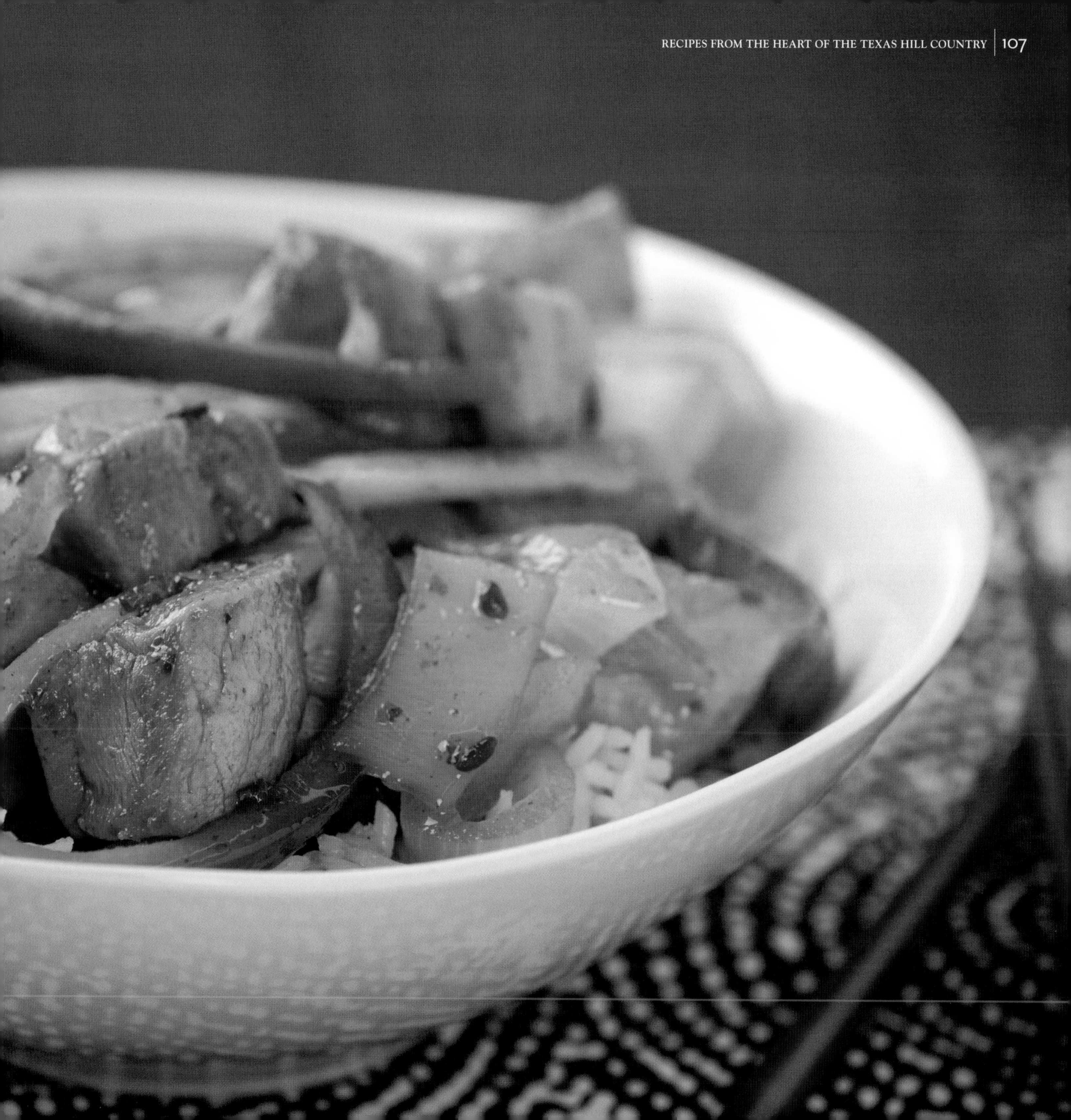

OVEN-BAKED *pomegranate* & *mango* CHIPOTLE RIBS

5 pounds pork spareribs (Baby-Back, St. Louis, or your choice)

Salt and pepper to taste

½–¾ cup Fischer & Wieser pomegranate & Mango Chipotle Sauce

If you like your ribs tender, juicy, and drippin' with sweet heat goodness, try this version built around the meeting of pomegranate and mango.

Preheat oven to 425° F. Line a shallow baking pan with nonstick foil. Place ribs, cut into 2–3 rib pieces, in baking pan, meaty side up; salt and pepper. Place in oven and roast for 20 minutes. Remove ribs from oven and reduce heat to 275° F. Turn ribs over so bony side is up. Drizzle Fischer & Wieser Pomegranate & Mango Chipotle Sauce over ribs; bake approximately 1 hour. Turn ribs over again, top with more sauce, and bake an additional hour. Allow ribs to sit for 7–10 minutes; serve with any unused Fischer & Wieser Pomegranate & Mango Chipotle Sauce on the side. 4–6 servings.

*Also use Fischer & Wieser Plum Chipotle Grilling Sauce, or Fischer & Wieser Roasted Blackberry Chipotle Sauce with this recipe.

PULLED PORK *with* *green* CHILES

1 pound pork butt, trimmed of fat

1 yellow onion, diced

1 tablespoon ground cumin

1 tablespoon garlic

2 bay leaves

2 tablespoons dried Mexican oregano

1 teaspoon salt

1 teaspoon black peppercorns

½ teaspoon cayenne pepper

1 small can whole mild green chiles, chopped ¼ inch

1 cup Fischer & Wieser Salsa Verde Ranchera

Within the beef-centric traditions of Texas barbecue, there is something of a pork tradition too. And we can think of few things more delicious than pulled pork taken South of the Border with our Fischer & Wieser Salsa Verde Ranchera.

Cook pork butt with bay leaves and peppercorns in boiling water for 1–1½ hours or until the pork falls apart. Skim the surface to remove any scum that forms, drain in a colander. Remove only the pork and shred. Saute the onion and garlic and add the shredded pulled pork. Add the cumin, Mexican oregano, cayenne, salt and green chiles to the pork mixture. Add Fischer & Wieser Salsa Verde Ranchera and cook over low heat until heated through, approximately 15 minutes. Serve hot with tortillas, diced tomatoes and sour cream. Serves 4.

pork

SWEET & SAVORY *onion* *glaze* PORK *chop* DINNER

2–3 tablespoons olive oil

Salt and Pepper to taste

6–8 pork chops

3–4 medium potatoes scrubbed, thinly sliced

½ –¾ cup chicken broth

1 cup half & half

1¾ cups Fischer & Wieser Sweet & Savory Onion Glaze

1 bag frozen green beans

¼ cup bacon bits

¼ cup French fried onion rings

For a one-dish meal that's full of flavor, with a creamy onion glaze sauce, you can't beat this casserole. We're betting it will become a staple around your house, the way it is around ours.

Add oil to pan; season the pork chops as desired; cook until almost done (no longer pink inside), 3–4 minutes per side. While chops are cooking, wash, scrub and thinly slice the potatoes; rinse and pat dry. Mix chicken broth, half & half and Fischer & Wieser Sweet & Savory Onion Glaze together. Spray 13" x 9" casserole with non-stick cooking spray. Pour some of the Fischer & Wieser Sweet & Savory Onion Glaze mixture into casserole, reserving remainder for later. Layer potatoes, green beans, and pork chops in casserole dish. Pour remainder of Fischer & Wieser Sweet & Savory Onion Glaze mixture over all. Cover with foil and place on a baking pan to avoid spilling. Bake at 400° F for 30–40 minutes. Last 10 minutes add bacon bits and French fried onion rings to top. Serves 6–8.

Whether golfing or serving up sandwiches with Fischer & Wieser award-winning sauces, both players and volunteers came together for a picture at the 2012 Nimitz Golf Classic. From left to right are Rebecca Rather, Phil Abel, Jenny Wieser, Ph.D., Deanna Fischer, Case D. Fischer, Dave Lewis, CPA, Elle Fischer, Simon Fischer and Dietz Fischer.

Mark Wieser showcases The Original Roasted Raspberry Chipotle Sauce® as a guest on WOAI in San Antonio.

Taking a break from the SIAL trade show in Paris, France where Fischer & Wieser showcased their international offerings are from left to right: Jonathan Pehl, Deanna Fischer, Jay Gans and Case D. Fischer.

pork

MOM'S *sausage &* *pepper* HOAGIE

1 pound fresh Italian pork sausage links, sweet (mild) or hot

½ cup water

1 tablespoon olive or other vegetable oil

1 medium green bell pepper, cut into thin strips

1 medium red bell pepper, cut into thin strips

1 large onion, sliced

½ teaspoon dried oregano

½ tablespoon chopped fresh basil

1 cup Mom's Special Marinara

4 hoagie rolls, split and toasted

Nothing could be better on a chilly fall or winter evening than these hearty sausage hoagies. A hoagie, in case you're wondering, is what some Yankees call a sub, a submarine sandwich or a grinder, which is more or less what our friends over in New Orleans call a po-boy. We just like to call it dang good!

Brown sausages, turning 2–3 times, in large skillet on medium heat for 5–10 minutes. Add water & bring to gentle simmer. Cover, reduce heat & continue simmering for 10 minutes. Drain sausages on paper towel. When cooled enough to handle, slice ¼–½ inch thick. If no oil or liquid remains in skillet, add up to 1 tablespoon oil. Increase heat to medium-high and add bell peppers, onion, oregano and basil. Cook, stirring frequently, until vegetables are crisp-tender (about 5 minutes). Return sausage to skillet and add the Mom's Special Marinara Pasta Sauce, then heat through. To serve, hollow out bottoms of rolls and place 1 sausage link in each depression. Top each with an equal amount of the vegetable mixture and serve. Serves 4.

EASY ITALIAN SAUSAGE *and* *pepperoni* PIZZA

1 (12 inch) pre-baked pizza crust

¾ cup Mom's Special Marinara

2 cups (8 ounces) shredded mozzarella cheese

½ cup thin-sliced onion

¾ cup thin-sliced green bell pepper

½ cup sliced ripe olives

3 ounces sliced pepperoni

3 ounces bulk-style Italian pork sausage, cooked and crumbled

¼ cup grated Parmesan cheese

Round up the family and have a pizza-making party. Using a pre-baked pizza crust takes most of the hard work out of it, but leaves most of the fun in.

Preheat oven to 400° F. Place pre-baked pizza crust on pizza pan. Spread the Mom's Special Marinara over the crust. Scatter the mozzarella cheese over the sauce, then repeat with remaining ingredients, except Parmesan cheese. Bake the pizza in preheated oven for 12–15 minutes, or until cheese is melted and bubbly. Remove from oven and scatter the Parmesan cheese over the top of the pizza before slicing into eight wedges with pizza cutter or sharp knife. Serve hot. Makes 8 slices.

Dietz Fischer making pizza in the Das Peach Haus kitchen in 2010.

pork

LINGUINE *with* ITALIAN SAUSAGE

1 pound Italian pork sausage links

20 ounces linguine pasta

6½ cups Mom's Spicy Arrabbiata

¼–½ cup grated Parmesan cheese

What a quick and easy way to come up with a hearty, spicy meal. The "spicy" comes from the Arrabiata, which is often translated as "angry." Trust us on this: you won't be!

Preheat oven to 350° F. Place sausage links on a baking sheet in a single layer. Bake in preheated oven for about 25 minutes (or until skin has turned completely brown). Place sausages on paper towels to drain, and then slice into bite-sized pieces. While sausage is baking, cook pasta according to package directions until tender. Drain well. Heat the Spicy Arrabbiata until hot. To serve, place a portion of the drained pasta on each serving plate. Ladle about one cup of the Spicy Arrabbiata over each serving of pasta. Arrange sliced sausage on each serving and scatter some of the Parmesan cheese over the top. Serves 4.

QUICK & EASY *lasagna with* MOM'S GARLIC & BASIL SPAGHETTI SAUCE

4½ cups Mom's Garlic & Basil Spaghetti Sauce

12 wide lasagna noodles, cooked al dente, drained well and laid out flat on a platter

1½ pounds link-style Italian pork sausage, cooked, drained and sliced about ¼ inch thick

1 pound ricotta cheese, crumbled

1 pound mozzarella cheese, shredded

1 cup grated Parmesan cheese

1 egg, beaten until frothy

Additional Parmesan cheese, grated

Lasagna is hard to beat when your appetite is begging for something rich, gooey and Italian. And what may have been an all-day labor of love for your Italian grandmother (which everyone should have or at least adopt!), it can be surprisingly quick and easy for you.

Preheat oven to 350° F. Lightly grease bottom and side of a 9" x 13" baking dish. Pour a thin layer of the Mom's Garlic & Basil Spaghetti Sauce into the bottom of the dish. Overlap four of the lasagna noodles lengthwise in the dish. Scatter half of the sliced Italian sausage over the noodles. Combine the three cheeses in a bowl and toss to blend well. Stir the beaten egg into the cheese mixture. Scatter half of the cheese over the sausage slices. Pour another layer of the spaghetti sauce over the cheese. Layer another four noodles and repeat with the remaining sausage and cheese layers. Pour another glaze of the sauce over the cheese. Place the final four noodles on top and pour the remaining sauce over the lasagna. Scatter a generous portion of grated Parmesan on top. Bake in preheated oven for about 35–40 minutes, or until cheese has melted and the dish is bubbly hot and lightly browned. Cut into desired portion sizes and serve hot. Serves 6–8.

beef

RECIPES

beef

beef

BEEF TACOS *with* FISCHER & WIESER *artichoke & olive* SALSA

1 pound lean ground beef

1 teaspoon salt

¼ teaspoon pepper

1 cup Fischer & Wieser Artichoke & Olive Salsa

8–12 taco shells

1 cup shredded iceberg lettuce

¾–1 cup diced tomato

2 sliced avocados

½ cup diced onion

½ cup sour cream

1 cup shredded Monterey Jack cheese

Love tacos? You'll love them even more with Fischer & Wieser Artichoke & Olive Salsa adding taste and texture to the familiar flavors. Not your everyday fare, but this will become an everyday favorite!

Brown beef with salt and pepper; drain fat. Add Fischer & Wieser Artichoke & Olive Salsa and heat through. Spoon ¼ cup of meat mixture down the center of each taco shell. Top with lettuce, tomato, avocado slice, onion, sour cream and Monterey Jack cheese. Serve with additional Fischer & Wieser Artichoke & Olive Salsa. Serves 4–6.

GRILLED RIBEYE STEAKS *with* *Big Bold* RED SOPPIN' *sauce*

4 (12 ounce) beef ribeye steaks

1½ cups Fischer & Wieser Big Bold Red Soppin' Sauce

Beef Rub (your choice)

Freshly ground black pepper

4 (½ inch thick) slices of real butter (not margarine)

Just coat your steaks with Fischer & Wieser Big Bold Red Soppin' Sauce—and slap 'em on the grill! You'll have dreams about these steaks!

Heat grill to medium-hot. Trim excess fat from edges of steaks. Pour Fischer & Wieser Big Bold Red Soppin' Sauce into a non-aluminum baking dish large enough to hold the four steaks in a single layer. Arrange steaks in the pan, coating bottoms with sauce. Turn steaks over and coat remaining side. When the grill is ready, remove steaks from pan and season liberally on both sides with beef rub. Place steaks on grill and grind a liberal amount of black pepper on each steak. Grill to desired degree of doneness; pepper the opposite side when steak is turned. Baste steaks with Fischer & Wieser Big Bold Red Soppin' Sauce as they cook. Just before removing steaks from the fire, lay one of the butter slices on top of each steak and cook just long enough for the butter to almost melt. Transfer steaks to serving plates. Serves 4.

beef

REBECCA RATHER'S *BBQ* *brisket* QUESADILLAS

BRISKET:

1 (3 pound) beef brisket

Salt and black pepper

1 teaspoon chili powder

2 cloves garlic, minced

1 (12 oz) can cola drink

MANGO BBQ SAUCE:

3 tablespoons olive oil

1 yellow onion, finely chopped

5 cloves garlic, minced

1 cup ketchup

¼ c. freshly squeezed lemon juice

3 tablespoons Worcestershire sauce

2 teaspoon Dijon mustard

1 teaspoon salt

1 teaspoon pepper

½ cup Fischer & Wieser Mango Ginger Habanero Sauce

QUESADILLA:

16 (8" diameter) flour tortillas

8 ounces brie cheese, thinly sliced with rind left on

1cup shredded Monterey jack cheese

For years, "Pastry Queen" Rebecca Rather operated a Fredericksburg destination that she cleverly called Rather Sweet. Here's her recipe for whipping up some quesdadillas to which every Texan has to sing, "These are a few of our favorite things."

Preheat oven to 325° F. Rub the meat with the salt, pepper, chili powder, and garlic; set it in a large ovenproof casserole dish. Pour the cola over it, cover the dish, and bake about 2 and 2½ hours, until tender. Turn the brisket over once during cooking, after 1½ hours. To make the sauce, heat olive oil in a large saute pan over medium heat. Saute the onion for 5 minutes. Add the garlic and saute 1 minute more. Stir in the ketchup, lemon juice, Worcestershire sauce, mustard, salt, pepper and mango sauce.

Cook sauce until heated through and puree it in a blender or food processor fitted with a metal blade. Measure 1 cup of the sauce for use in the quesadilla; the remaining sauce can be refrigerated in a glass jar up to 1 week.

Remove brisket from its cooking liquid and trim off any visible fat. Slice about half of the brisket against the grain; remaining brisket can be wrapped and frozen. Set a large frying pan or griddle on medium-high heat and coat with a thin layer of cooking spray. Lay 2 tortillas on the griddle and cover each with 3–4 slices of brisket and the brie, ¼ cup Monterey jack and a spoonful of the sauce. Top with 2 tortillas. Grill the quesadillas until the bottoms are crisp and golden brown. Cut into quarters and serve on a large plate or platter. Serves 4.

SMOKEHOUSE *bacon* BRISKET

1 (3–5 pound) center cut brisket, trimmed

1 cup Fischer & Wieser All Purpose Vegetable & Meat Marinade

1½ cups Fischer & Wieser Smokehouse Bacon & Chipotle Grilling Sauce

1–2 teaspoons fajita seasoning (or salt and pepper)

1 tablespoon flour

1 large onion, sliced

1 large browning bag

This way of preparing brisket is the easiest ever, and produces the tenderest, smokiest and, yes, baconiest slice of barbecued beef you'll every try.

This recipe is also terrific with Texas Pit BBQ Sauce.

Pour ½ cup Fischer & Wieser All Purpose Vegetable & Meat Marinade in shallow casserole dish (13" x 9"). Place brisket in dish; pour remainder of Fischer & Wieser All Purpose Vegetable & Meat Marinade over brisket. Cover tightly and place in refrigerator to marinate 12 hours, turning several times as convenient. After marinating, remove brisket from casserole, discard marinade, wash casserole. Set oven at 250° F. Flour large browning bag, place in casserole; pour ½ cup Fischer & Wieser Smokehouse Bacon & Chipotle Grilling Sauce into bottom of bag, mixing into flour. Place onion slices on bottom of bag. Set brisket in bag on top of onions. Pour ½ cup more Fischer & Wieser Smokehouse Bacon & Chipotle Grilling Sauce over brisket. Sprinkle with fajita seasoning or salt and pepper. Close bag, puncture with a fork as directed on package, place casserole in oven and cook 4–6 hours, or until brisket is very tender when a fork is inserted in thickest part. Slice across the grain; serve hot. Serves 6.

GRILLED *venison* LOIN *from* NAVAJO GRILL*

VENISON:
1½–2 pounds venison backstrap (loin)
Salt and freshly ground black pepper
3 cloves of garlic
1 large sprig of rosemary
½ cup olive oil

BALSAMIC GLAZE:
½ cup balsamic vinegar
½ cup red wine
¼ cup honey
¼ teaspoon red pepper flakes
½ tablespoon rosemary

SAUTEED KALE:
1 bunch good-quality kale, washed,
lightly shaken and shredded,
with stems removed
4 cloves garlic, sliced
2 tablespoons butter or olive oil
1 wedge of lime
Salt and pepper

2 cups cooked faro, or other grain

For more than a decade now, Navajo Grill has shined as one of Fredericksburg's most ambitious and most successful restaurants, finding the perfect balance between sophisticated food and all the casual comfort and friendliness of a small Texas town. Executive chef Josh Raymer, whose father Mike got things rolling at the restaurant, was kind enough to share this recipe for venison loin, also known (especially among Texas hunters) as backstrap.

At least 2 hours before service, and preferably the day before you plan to serve, lightly salt and pepper the venison. Smash the garlic and bruise the rosemary by rubbing it in your hands. Combine with the olive oil in a tight-fitting container so the oil can circulate around the meat. Allow to marinate.

Prepare the Balsamic Glaze: Bring all ingredients to a boil in a stainless steel sauce pot, then reduce heat and simmer till liquid reduces by about half. It should just coat the back of spoon. Prepare the Sauteed Kale: In a large pan over low heat, add butter and garlic, slowly cooking till the garlic just starts to color. Turn the garlic till it is colored evenly and softened. Turn the heat to high as the butter browns. Toss in the kale; it will crackle. Quickly toss the kale in a hot pan, adding lime juice. Season to taste. Fresh kale doesn't need much acid or salt, just enough to enhance its natural flavor.

When ready, preheat gas or wood-fired grill. Season again with salt and pepper. Grill on all sides until internal temperature reaches about 110° F, about 8 minutes, then remove from heat and allow to rest so juices can redistribute evenly, 6–8 minutes. Internal temperature should rise to 120° F or 130° F, a nice medium rare. Slice the meat against the grain about ¼ inch thick and brush the slices with the balsamic glaze. Serve with cooked faro and sauteed kale. Serves 4.

SPICY *garlic* STEAK *& grilling* SAUCE BURGERS

6 (6 ounce) burger patties

1–1½ cups Fischer & Wieser Spicy Garlic Steak & Grilling Sauce

Freshly cracked black pepper, to taste

Ground red pepper, to taste

6 slices asadero cheese

12 pats butter, melted

6–12 slices tomatoes

6–12 leaves iceberg lettuce

6 good-quality burger buns

Melted butter

The flavors in Fischer & Wieser Spicy Garlic Steak & Grilling Sauce are perfect for burgers. Try this at your next family cookout.

Heat a grill to medium hot. Pour 1 cup of the Fischer & Wieser Spicy Garlic Steak & Grilling Sauce in a baking dish. Place the burger patties in the sauce, turning to coat both sides well. Salt and pepper to taste. Grill the burgers on the grill to desired degree of doneness, basting them with more Fischer & Wieser Spicy Garlic Steak & Grilling Sauce each time you turn them. About 3–4 minutes before the burgers are done, place a slice of cheese on top of each burger. Open the buns and paint the insides with melted butter. Place buns, buttered sides down, on the grill rack; grill buns just long enough to lightly brown, with edges slightly crisp. Place a burger on each bun. Layer on tomato slices and lettuce leaves. Serves 6.

beef

GRILLED TEXASBURGERS *with* *Big Bold* RED SOPPIN' *sauce* *and* CHIPOTLE *chile* KETCHUP

6 (6 ounce) burger patties

1–1½ cups Fischer & Wieser Big Bold Red Soppin' Sauce

Freshly cracked black pepper

Ground red pepper to taste

6 slices asadero cheese

12 pats butter, melted

½ cup Fischer & Wieser Chipotle Chile Ketchup

6 good quality burger buns

Melted butter

6–12 slices tomatoes

6–12 leaves iceberg lettuce

6–12 thinly sliced onions

We're in Texas. We use soppin' sauce. And Fischer & Wieser's is THE BEST! You also can't beat our Chipotle Chile Ketchup—just maybe the best condiment on the planet. Like we say in Texas: It ain't braggin' if it's true.

Heat a grill to medium hot. Pour 1 cup of the Fischer & Wieser Big Bold Red Soppin' Sauce in a baking dish. Place the burger patties in the sauce, turning to coat both sides well. Salt and pepper to taste. Grill the burgers on the grill to desired degree of doneness, basting them with more Fischer & Wieser Big Bold Red Soppin' Sauce each time you turn them. About 3–4 minutes before the burgers are done, place a slice of cheese on top of each burger. Open the buns and paint the insides with melted butter. Place buns, buttered sides down, on the grill rack; grill buns just long enough to lightly brown, with edges slightly crisp. Place a burger on each bun and pour some of the Fischer & Wieser Chipotle Chile Ketchup on top. Layer on tomato slices, lettuce leaves and onion slices. Serves 6.

SPICY *garlic* STEAK *& grilling sauce* RIBEYE ROAST

There's really nothing better than a ribeye roast—and especially when you add our Spicy Garlic Steak & Grilling Sauce.

1 teaspoon black pepper

2 teaspoons onion salt

2 teaspoons garlic salt

2 teaspoons hickory smoke salt

1 teaspoon minced fresh rosemary

4 pound bone in ribeye roast

1¾ cup Fischer & Wieser Spicy Garlic Steak & Grilling Sauce

In a small bowl, mix black pepper, onion salt, garlic salt, hickory smoke salt, and rosemary. Rub ribeye with mixture. Sear all four sides of roast on a high heat. Place meat on a medium heat pit or smoker with bone side up. Using a grill thermometer, grill roast for 2 hours at 250° F. The last 3–5 minutes of cook time, continuously glaze meat with Fischer & Wieser Spicy Garlic Steak & Grilling Sauce. Serve with green beans and baked potatoes. Serves 6–8.

SWEET & SAVORY *onion glaze* BURGERS

8½ pound burger patties, pre-formed

Salt and pepper to taste

1 cup Fischer & Wieser Sweet & Savory Onion Glaze

8 ea hamburger buns

8 slices cheese

Lettuce, tomatoes, onions, pickles, etc.

Tasty burgers always make friends. Use this recipe to make some new ones.

On a gas grill over medium heat, start grilling burgers. Season each side with salt and pepper while cooking. Flip the burgers every 3–5 minutes until cooked to your desired doneness. About two flips each side should be enough for a medium doneness. On the last flip glaze burgers with the Fischer & Wieser Sweet & Savory Onion Glaze and caramelize. Lightly toast buns on the upper rack while the burgers are grilling. No rack? No problem! Quickly toast buns on the actual grill, but be fast! This method goes very quickly. Place cheese on burgers and allow to melt. Let guests dress to suit. Serves 8.

beef

SPICY SESAME *grilled* *sirloin* KEBABS

1–1½ pounds beef sirloin, cubed

1 cup Fischer & Wieser Spicy Sesame Stir Fry & Dipping Sauce

1 green bell pepper, cut into 1" x 1" pieces

1 red bell pepper, cut into 1" x 1" pieces

1 medium onion, cut in half, then into wedges and separated

2 cups sliced large mushrooms

Tender, juicy and delicious—those will be just some of the adjectives your guests will use to describe these fantastic skewers of grilled meat.

Start coals in charcoal grill to allow to die down while preparing shish ka-bobs. Cut beef into cubes. Pour Fischer & Wieser Spicy Sesame Stir Fry & Dipping Sauce over beef cubes and marinate 20–30 minutes. Cut up vegetables. After beef has marinated the allotted time, thread beef & vegetables onto skewers (if using bamboo, soak in water while meat is marinating). When coals are ready, grill shish ka-bobs 12–15 minutes, or until beef juices run clear when pierced. Brush with Fischer & Wieser Spicy Sesame Stir Fry & Dipping Sauce 2–3 times per side while grilling. Serve with rice, if desired. Serves 6.

beef

EASY *salsa* CHILI

1 pound ground beef

¼ cup chopped onion

4 cups Fischer & Wieser Black Bean
& Corn Salsa

2 tablespoons chili powder

½ teaspoon garlic powder (optional)

2 cups shredded Mexican cheese

That's the name our staff gave this dish when it was tested by our chef. Another name—"Beer drinkin' chili!" Just 10 minutes and it's in the crockpot, ready to simmer until you're ready to eat. Here in Texas, we don't usually put any beans in our chili—but we have it on good authority that throwing in some cooked kidney, pintos or black beans would taste real good too. We won't tell if you won't.

Brown ground beef and chopped onion in heavy skillet over medium heat. Drain. Pour beef and onion mixture into slow cooker. Add Fischer & Wieser Black Bean & Corn Salsa, chili powder and garlic powder (if desired). Set slow cooker on high and cook 3 hours, or low and cook 6 hours. Serve with tortilla chips, shredded Mexican cheese, and sour cream if desired. Serves 4–6.

Love tacos? You'll love them even more with Fischer & Wieser Black Bean & Corn Salsa complementing the flavors.

BEEF TACOS *with* FISCHER & WIESER *black bean &* corn SALSA

When you gotta have something quick and hearty, these multi-textured Southwestern tacos fill the bill.

1 pound lean ground beef

1 teaspoon salt

¼ teaspoon pepper

1 cup Fischer & Wieser Black Bean & Corn Salsa

8–12 taco shells

1 cup shredded iceberg lettuce

¾ - 1 cup diced tomato

2 sliced avocados

½ cup diced onion

½ cup sour cream

1 cup shredded Monterey Jack cheese

Brown beef, seasoning with salt and pepper; drain fat. Add Fischer & Wieser Black Bean & Corn Salsa and heat through. Spoon ¼ cup of meat mixture down the center of each taco shell. Top with lettuce, tomato, avocado slice, onion, sour cream and Monterey Jack cheese. Serve with additional Fischer & Wieser Black Bean & Corn Salsa. Serves 4–6.

TAMALE, *black* BEAN *& corn* CASSEROLE

1 16 ounce package ready-made beef (or pork, if you prefer) tamales

1 (10 ounce) package frozen white or yellow corn

1 (16 ounce) can black beans, drained

1 (4 ounce) can diced mild green chilies

3 green onions, chopped

1 cup chopped fresh cilantro

1 cup whipping cream

1 cup Fischer & Wieser Guacamole Starter–Just Add Avocadoes

1½ teaspoons chili powder

1 teaspoon ground cumin

½ teaspoon salt

¼ teaspoon ground black pepper

2 (8 ounce) packages shredded Monterey Jack cheese

GARNISH:
Avocado slices

Black olives

Additional Fischer & Wieser Guacamole Starter–Just Add Avocadoes

Sour cream

Cilantro

Rave reviews are what you'll reap with this casserole, thanks to its spicy flavor combination of green chiles, cilantro and tamales.

Preheat oven to 375° F. Spray medium casserole dish with non-stick cooking spray. Remove husks from tamales; cut in half lengthwise. Place tamales in single layer in medium casserole dish. Sprinkle with frozen corn, black beans, chilies, green onions and ½ cup chopped cilantro. Whisk cream, Fischer & Wieser Guacamole Starter–Just Add Avocadoes, chili powder, cumin, salt and pepper, and 1 package Monterey Jack shredded cheese in medium bowl to blend. Drizzle over casserole. Sprinkle remainder of cheese over the top. Serves 8–12.

Bake casserole uncovered until heated through and bubbling, about 35 minutes. Sprinkle with ½ cup more cilantro, if desired for garnish. Serve with avocado, sour cream, black olives and more Fischer & Wieser Guacamole Starter–Just Add Avocados as well. Serves 8–12.

beef

BEEF *or* CHICKEN *fajitas*

1 (2 pound) beef skirt steak or 4 boneless, skinless chicken breasts

¼ cup Fischer & Wieser All Purpose Vegetable & Meat Marinade

Fajita seasoning, or salt and pepper, to taste

16 flour or corn tortillas, as desired

2 cups shredded iceberg, Romaine, or curly leaf lettuce

½ purple onion, diced

1 tomato, diced

¾ cup shredded Monterey Jack Cheese

½–¾ cup Fischer & Wieser Salsa a la Charra

GARNISHES:

Guacamole*

Sour cream

Black olives

Sliced avocados

Whether you use beef, chicken or both, these fajitas are muy delicioso! They're great eatin', as well as great fun to grill while your friends are gathered round chompin' at the bit for a taste.

Prepare grill for cooking. Marinate skirt steak or chicken breasts in Fischer & Wieser All Purpose Vegetable and Meat Marinade 15 minutes (or longer, as time allows). Sprinkle with fajita seasoning or salt and pepper to taste. Grill skirt steak until meat thermometer inserted in thickest part reaches 145° F for 15 seconds; grill chicken breasts until meat thermometer inserted in thickest part reaches 165° for 15 seconds. When done, remove to cutting board and slice into ½" slices. Heat tortillas on griddle or microwave (wrap in paper towel and heat 25 seconds or so, depending on your microwave). To serve, place warmed tortillas, lettuces, onion, tomato, cheese and Fischer & Wieser Gourmet Salsa A La Charra in serving containers. Allow guests to prepare their fajitas as they desire. Add garnishes as desired. Serves 8.

* Need a quick way to make guacamole for this recipe? Peel, pit and roughly mash 3 medium avocados in large mixing bowl. Add ½ cup Fischer & Wieser Just Add Avocados–Guacamole Starter. Mix and serve. Serves 8–12.

ROAST BEEF *sandwich with* *sweet heat* MUSTARD DIPPIN' *sauce*

What're you gonna' fix when time is short and the guys (and gals) are starvin'? This fantastic hoagie's the answer. You'll want to keep our Sweet Heat Mustard on hand for all kinds of sandwiches after you taste this.

¼–½ cup mayonnaise

¼ cup Fischer & Wieser Sweet Heat Mustard

6 hoagie buns, split

1½–2 pounds deli sliced roast beef

2 tomatoes, thinly sliced

½ red onion, thinly sliced

12 slices provolone cheese

1 small can sliced black olives

Salt and pepper to taste

Mix mayonnaise and Fischer & Wieser Sweet Heat Mustard together. Cut rolls in half. Place on a baking sheet. Spread rolls with mayonnaise and Fischer & Wieser Sweet Heat Mustard mixture. Layer with roast beef, tomato, red onion, provolone, black olives, and salt and pepper. Broil 3–6 inches from heat source for 2–4 minutes (keep a constant eye on it) until cheese is bubbly and beginning to brown. Serve with extra mayonnaise and Fischer & Wieser Sweet Heat Mustard mixture as dippin' sauce. Serves 6.

OLD-FASHIONED *Texas pit BBQ* BURGERS

3 pounds lean ground chuck

1½ teaspoons freshly ground black pepper (or fajita seasoning)

½ cup dehydrated onion flakes

¼ cup Fischer & Wieser Texas Pit BBQ Sauce

Additional Fischer & Wieser Texas Pit BBQ Sauce for basting

GARNISHES:

Sliced tomatoes

Lettuce leaves

Pickles

Avocados

Crisp Bacon

Cheddar Cheese

Sliced onions

If you want a good old-fashioned Texas burger, look no further than this recipe. Not surprisingly, a few generations of extra goodness arrives with the sauce.

Preheat gas char grill to medium heat. In a large bowl combine the ground chuck, black pepper or fajita seasoning, dehydrated onion flakes and ¼ cup of Fischer & Wieser Texas Pit BBQ Sauce. Using your hands, blend the mixture well, distributing ingredients thoroughly. Separate the meat mixture into 8 equal portions; pat meat into firm burgers. Place burgers on preheated grill and cook, basting with additional Fischer & Wieser Texas Pit BBQ Sauce each time you turn them, for about 8 minutes per side. To serve, assemble burgers with your favorite condiments. Serves 8.

SUGGESTED CONDIMENTS: Sliced tomatoes, lettuce leaves, pickles, avocados, crisp bacon, cheddar cheese, sliced onions.

beef

MOM'S *meatloaf*

1 cup fine fresh bread crumbs

⅓ cup whole milk

2 large eggs

1 pound ground chuck

⅔ pound ground pork (not lean)

12 ounces Mom's Special Marinara Pasta Sauce

1 teaspoon salt (or more if desired)

2 teaspoons freshly ground black pepper

⅓ cup finely chopped flat-leaf parsley

Looking for a great meatloaf that also makes great sandwiches, if there's any left over? This is so good, there actually might not be any left over.

Preheat oven to 350° F. In a bowl, soak bread crumbs in milk. Beat the eggs lightly with a fork. Add the beef, pork, eggs, 4 ounces (½ cup) pasta sauce, salt, pepper, and parsley. Mix thoroughly with hands and pack into 9" x 5" loaf pan. Bake for one hour; drain, then top with 4 ounces (½ cup) of the remaining pasta sauce. Return to oven until meat thermometer inserted in center reads 155° F, about 10–12 more minutes. Let stand 10 minutes. Heat any leftover sauce and serve on the side. NOTE: Meatloaf can keep up to 3 days in the refrigerator after cooking. Leftovers can be reheated and served with remaining sauce or in a meatloaf sandwich. Serves 4–6

NOTE: Any of our Mom's pasta sauces can be used with this recipe!

beef

HOT BEEF *melt grilled* PIZZA

1 (12 inch) prepared pizza crust

1 teaspoon olive oil

½ teaspoon poppy seeds

4 ounces pasteurized prepared cheese product, cubed

¼ teaspoon crushed red pepper flakes

⅔ cup Mom's Special Marinara

2.5 ounce deli roast beef, cut paper thin and sliced into ¼ inch strips

½ cup green pepper, small diced

⅓ cup red onions, small diced

1 cup smoked provolone or smoked mozzarella cheese, shredded

Grilled pizza has to be an idea whose time has come, and we have to thank good customer Dianna Wara of Washington, IL, for her wonderful recipe.

Preheat grill on medium-high heat (10–15 minutes). Brush the rim of the pizza crust with olive oil and sprinkle on the poppy seeds evenly around the rim. In a microwave-safe bowl, add pasteurized prepared cheese product and red pepper flakes. Melt in microwave. Stir and then spread the cheese mix evenly over pizza crust, avoiding rim. In a medium sized bowl, mix the Mom's Special Marinara and roast beef strips together. Spread saucy roast beef evenly over the top of the pizza crust. Next, layer green peppers, onions, and smoked provolone or smoked mozzarella cheese. Place pizza on grill and close lid. Cook for 10–15 minutes or until cheese has melted and bottom crust is gold in color. Remove from grill, slice and serve! 6–8 slices.

GOOD OLD *fashioned spaghetti* 'n' *meatballs* WITH MOM'S GARLIC & BASIL *spaghetti sauce*

MEATBALLS:

½ pound lean ground beef

½ pound bulk-style Italian sausage

1 medium onion, finely chopped

4 large garlic cloves, minced

½ teaspoon crushed red pepper flakes

1 teaspoon salt

1 teaspoon freshly ground black pepper

3 (1 inch thick) slices French bread, torn into tiny bits

⅓ cup grated Parmesan cheese

2 eggs, beaten

½ cup extra virgin olive oil

⅓ cup dry Vermouth

3 cups Mom's Garlic & Basil Spaghetti Sauce

20 ounces spaghetti, cooked al dente and well drained

Grated Parmesan cheese

Spaghetti 'n' Meatballs is one of those comfort foods we never seem to tire of. The meatballs take a little time, but they can be done ahead and even frozen. The hard part for our "Moms" used to be making the spaghetti sauce. Not anymore.

Begin by making the Meatballs, combining the ground beef and Italian sausage in a large bowl. Add the onion, minced garlic, red pepper flakes, salt and pepper. Stir to blend well. Using your hands, work the torn bread and Parmesan cheese into the meat mixture, blending well. Stir in the beaten eggs, incorporating them well. Form the meat mixture into 18 meatballs; refrigerate, covered, until ready to use.

Heat the olive oil in a heavy 12 inch, deep-sided skillet over medium heat. Add the meatballs in a single layer and cook until well browned on the bottom before turning, about 7–8 minutes. Continue to cook, turning meatballs often, until they are cooked through, about 15 minutes. Carefully pour off all fat from the pan, then return pan to medium heat.

Whisk the Vermouth into the Mom's Garlic & Basil Spaghetti Sauce, then stir the sauce into the pan, carefully scraping up the browned bits of meat glaze from the bottom of the pan. Take care not to break up the meatballs. Turn heat to medium-low, cover the pan and cook for 15 minutes. To serve, place a portion of the cooked spaghetti on each plate and top with 3 or 4 meatballs. Spoon some of the sauce over each portion and scatter with grated Parmesan cheese. Serves 4–6.

beef

ITALIAN *cubed* STEAKS

1 stick (½ cup) butter or margarine

¼ cup chopped onion

¼ cup chopped green pepper

4 beef cube steaks, sliced into 1 inch strips

Salt and pepper to taste

Water or beef broth as needed

3 cups Mom's Garlic & Basil Spaghetti Sauce

For an easy gourmet entree, try this slow-simmered Italian offering. Serve over pasta or rice, with a green salad and Italian bread.

Melt butter in skillet; add chopped onion, green pepper, sliced seasoned cube steaks. Saute until onions are translucent and steaks are browned, approximately 10 minutes. Pour Mom's Garlic & Basil Spaghetti Sauce over ingredients in skillet. Bring to a boil and reduce heat to simmer. Add water or beef broth ¼ cup at a time as needed. Simmer 2 hours or until cube steak is tender.

Alternatively, if desired, place a liner in large capacity slow cooker; place browned steak, onions, peppers in liner. Pour Mom's Garlic & Basil Spaghetti Sauce over all, and set slow cooker on low. Cook for 8–10 hours, until steak is very tender. Serve over pasta or rice. Serves 4.

NOTE: Mom's Organic Garlic & Basil Pasta Sauce, Mom's Organic Roasted Pepper also work well with this recipe.

MEXITALIAN *chiligetti*

1 pound ground beef, browned and drained

½ medium onion, chopped

1 small package spaghetti, uncooked

1 can red beans

4 cups Mom's Spicy Arrabiata

2 tablespoons Worcestershire Sauce

1 cup water

Both words in the name of this dish may strike you as strange, but there's nothing all that strange about this delicious meeting of two of our favorite food cultures.

Heat oven to 350° F. Brown ground beef and onions in medium skillet; drain. Spray 13" x 9" rectangular casserole with non-stick cooking spray. Place 1 layer of ground beef & onion mixture, 1 layer of spaghetti, 1 layer of beans in casserole; repeat until all ingredients are used. Mix Mom's Spicy Arrabiata, Worcestershire Sauce, and water together. Stir well. Pour over casserole ingredients. Bake in preheated oven 45–60 minutes, or until liquid is absorbed and spaghetti is done. Serves 8–12.

beef

TOMATO *basil* SOUP
pasta DINNER

4 tablespoons olive oil

16 prepared meatballs

4 cups Mom's Limited Edition Tomato Basil Soup

8 cups cooked pasta of your preference

1 cup grated parmesan or mozzarella cheese

Want a quick way to make a pasta meatball dinner? Just ask your Mom! In this case, it may be quicker to open a jar of our Limited Edition Tomato Basil Soup. Then you can simply invite your Mom over to enjoy the finished product.

Brown meatballs in olive oil in skillet over medium-high heat. Drain. Pour Mom's Limited Edition Tomato Basil Soup over meatballs in skillet. Allow to simmer 20–30 minutes. While meatballs are simmering, prepare pasta according to package directions. Serve meatballs over pasta. Sprinkle with cheese, as desired. Serves 4.

STEPPED UP *ultimate* *garlic* FLANK STEAK

2 pounds flank steak, flattened with mallet

1 cup chopped scallions

Salt and black pepper to taste

1 cup Fischer & Wieser Spicy Garlic Steak & Grilling Sauce

1 cup dry sherry

1 tablespoon maple syrup

½ cup tomato paste

Summer grilling—you just gotta love it. Based on this recipe, our good customer Wolfgang Hanau of West Palm Beach, FL, sure does!

Spread flattened flank steak with scallions, salt and pepper. Combine remaining ingredients into a marinade. Roll up flank steak; marinate 1–2 hours or as long as you wish (for intense flavor), slice into pin wheels, skewer, grill, occasionally basting with marinade. Serves 4.

RECIPES

side dishes

SPICY GERMAN *potato* SALAD

This really tasty potato salad is the essence of the Texas Hill Country with the bold, underlying taste of whole grain mustard and just a hint of spice.

10 medium–sized new potatoes, about two pounds, halved and sliced into bite–sizes pieces

3 hard-boiled eggs, peeled and chopped

3 green onions, chopped, including green tops

⅓ cup Fischer & Wieser Sweet, Sour & Smokey Mustard Sauce

¼ cup mayonnaise

¼ cup dill relish

Place sliced potatoes in a heavy 4 quart saucepan; add cold water to cover. Bring the potatoes to a boil over medium heat; cook until potatoes are tender, about 18–20 minutes. Drain potatoes in colander and run under cold water until they are cool enough to handle. Transfer potatoes to a medium–sized bowl; add chopped eggs and green onions. In a separate bowl, combine Fischer & Wieser Sweet, Sour & Smokey Mustard Sauce, mayonnaise and dill relish; stir until well blended. Fold the sauce mixture into the potatoes, coating well. Refrigerate until well chilled before serving. Serves 4–6.

FISCHER & WIESER *all purpose vegetable* & MEAT MARINADE GRILLED *veggies*

Whole carrots, peeled, thin, tapered ends removed

Baking potatoes, (skin on), cut lengthwise into ½ inch thick slices, or tiny red new potatoes, cut in half

Eggplant (skin on), cut lengthwise into ½ inch thick slices

Sliced red or yellow onions

Bell peppers, seeds and veins removed, cut into fourths

Roma tomatoes, cut in half lengthwise

Small zucchini and yellow squash, halved lengthwise

Beets, peeled and sliced into ¼ inch thick slices

Green onions, whole, with roots and tender tops removed

Greens (bok choy, collards, mustard, kale, Swiss chard, romaine)

1½ cups Fischer & Wieser All Purpose Vegetable & Meat Marinade

If you're looking for a new way to prepare those oh-so-nutritious veggies, try Fischer & Wieser All Purpose Vegetable & Meat Marinade, and then grill.

Select the vegetables you wish to grill and place them in a single layer in a baking pan. Pour a liberal amount of the Fischer & Wieser All Purpose Vegetable & Meat Marinade on the vegetables, turning them to coat all sides. Marinate for 1 hour at room temperature. Grill the vegetables on gas grill over medium heat. The different vegetables will take various lengths of time grill. Carrots will take about 20–30 minutes, while the zucchini and yellow squash will take about 5–8 minutes. Grill just until the vegetables are browned and caramelized, but not charred. Turn often, basting with the Fischer & Wieser All Purpose Vegetable & Meat Marinade left in the pan. Serve hot.

BAKED BEANS *with* FISCHER & WIESER *chipotle chile* KETCHUP

2 (15 ounce) cans pork and beans

¾ cup Fischer & Wieser Chipotle Chile Ketchup

¼ cup light brown sugar

½ cup onion, chopped

Looking for the perfect side dish for your casual backyard cookout? This one's a winner—and so easy, using canned beans and our great subtly spicy Fischer & Wieser Chipotle Chile Ketchup.

Preheat oven to 350° F. Combine all ingredients in a 3 quart ovenproof casserole dish. Stir to blend well and break up any lumps of brown sugar. Place the casserole in the oven and bake for 30–45 minutes, or until bubbly and slightly thickened. Serve hot. Serves 4–6.

CILANTRO PEPITO *pesto* *Roma* TOMATOES

6 large Roma tomatoes, cut in half lengthwise

Salt

¾ cup Fischer & Wieser Cilantro Pepito Pesto Appetizer-Spread

1 cup shredded Romano cheese

This is great with roasted or grilled red meats, or, for a unique party finger good, substitute halved cherry tomatoes.

Preheat broiler; place oven rack 6 inches below heat source. Line a baking sheet with parchment paper; set aside. Using a grapefruit knife or melon baller, remove about 2 teaspoons of pulp from each tomato half. Lightly salt each tomato and place on prepared baking sheet. Spoon heaping tablespoon of Fischer & Wieser Cilantro Pepito Pesto Appetizer-Spread into each tomato half. Top each portion with some of the grated Romano cheese. Place baking sheet under preheated broiler and cook until cheese is lightly browned and tomatoes are slightly wilted, about 3–5 minutes. Serve hot. Serves 4–6.

Case D. Fischer and Mark Wieser check the early peaches of the 2012 season.

Handcrafting one jar at a time, Case D. Fischer makes Apple Butter for Oktoberfest in 1979.

Fischer & Wieser hosted the Jelly Jamboree in 2005 at Das Peach Haus®, including other Gillespie Country produce growers such as the Studebaker family.

Jack Henderson and Dietz and Simon Fischer make wearable signs to drive peach traffic during the summer of 2010, the best peach crop in Mark Wieser's lifetime.

!ESPECIAL! *pasilla* CHILE *baked* CHEESE GRITS

Quick grits, 4 servings

4 ounces pasteurized process cheese, cut into ½ inch cubes

6 slices peppered bacon, cooked until crisp, drained and chopped fine

6 green onions, chopped, including green tops

1 egg, beaten

½ cup Fischer & Wieser ¡Especial! Pasilla Chile Finishing Sauce

No other side dish says Texas quite like this one. The creamy grits are enhanced with the savory addition of cheddar cheese, then spiked up Texas-level with the sultry smoky flavor of this Fischer & Wieser finishing sauce.

Preheat oven to 350° F. Lightly butter a 9" x 13" baking dish; set aside. Cook the grits according to package directions. Remove from heat and quickly whisk in the cheese, chopped bacon and green onions until cheese is melted and well blended. Whisk in the beaten egg and Fischer & Wieser ¡Especial! Pasilla Chile Finishing Sauce. Turn mixture out into prepared baking dish and bake in preheated oven for about 45 minutes, or until top is lightly browned and grits are set. Serve hot. Serves 4.

side dishes

SWEET HEAT *mustard* & BACON *creamed* SMASHED POTATOES

2½ pounds small red new potatoes, unpeeled, quartered

½ cup Fischer & Wieser Sweet Heat Mustard

½ cup whipping cream

3 tablespoons unsalted butter, melted

6 slices applewood-smoked bacon, cooked until crisp, then crumbled

1–2 teaspoons sea salt

¼ teaspoon freshly ground black pepper

Parsley sprigs for garnish

Talk about your comfort food—this potato dish with crumbled bacon is definitely it. Try with a side of ham or brisket.

Place the unpeeled potato quarters in a heavy 6 quart saucepan. Add cold water to cover and bring to a boil over medium high heat. Simmer until potatoes are very soft, about 20 minutes. While potatoes are cooking, combine the Fischer & Wieser Sweet Heat Mustard, whipping cream, melted butter and crumbled bacon in a medium sized bowl. Whisk to blend well; set aside. Drain the potatoes in a colander and immediately return them to the pan. Using a potato masher, smash the potatoes, leaving them a little chunky. Stir in the mustard mixture, blending well. Add salt and black pepper to taste. Serve hot. Garnish with parsley sprigs. Serves 6–8.

SEARED BUTTON *mushrooms* with TRADITIONAL STEAK & GRILLING *sauce*

What a treat to accompany grilled steak! Better make plenty, because you'll have your family or guests asking for more.

¼ cup unsalted butter

12 ounces small whole button mushrooms

½ teaspoon freshly ground black pepper

1 cup Fischer & Wieser Traditional Steak & Grilling Sauce

Melt butter in heavy 12" skillet over medium-high heat. When butter is foaming hot, add mushrooms & black pepper. Cook, stirring often, until mushroom liquid has evaporated and only butter remains in the skillet, about 8–10 minutes. Stir in the Fischer & Wieser Traditional Steak & Grilling Sauce, blending well. Cook, stirring constantly, until sauce has thickened and mushrooms are lightly browned. Serve hot over grilled steaks. Serves 6–8.

BAKED PENNE *with* MOM'S *Puttanesca* SAUCE

1 pound penne pasta, cooked al dente and well drained, or substitute your favorite tubular pasta

1 cup (4 ounces) shredded Asiago cheese

3 cups Mom's Puttanesca Sauce

⅓ cup breadcrumbs

Looking for that perfect side dish to pair with your entree? This easy-to-prepare pasta dish is ready in a flash with little muss or fuss.

Preheat oven to 350° F. Place the well drained pasta in a large bowl. Toss with the Asiago cheese and stir in the jar of Mom's Puttanesca Sauce. Turn the pasta out into a 9" x 12" baking dish; sprinkle with bread crumbs. Bake in preheated oven for 30 minutes, or until cheese has melted and sauce is bubbly. Serve hot. Serves 4.

GRILLED *veggies*

1–1½ pounds small red or white potatoes, washed and halved

2 each yellow squash, green peppers, and onions

1–1½ pounds fresh green beans

1–2 cups Fischer & Wieser Sweet & Savory Onion Glaze

Meats aren't the only things we grill in Texas, as this recipe from good customer Donna Reed of Cleveland, TX, makes clear.

Wash and prep vegetables. Slice squash and peppers; quarter onions; cut ends off green beans. Place all veggies in a single layer on a doubled sheet of heavy duty aluminum foil. Pour Fischer & Wieser Sweet & Savory Onion Glaze evenly over all vegetables. Using doubled foil, cover veggies and "seal" edges tightly. Grill on low fire, or towards edge of grill, until veggies are tender. (Test with fork through top layer of foil after about 25–35 minutes, depending on heat). Serves 6.

GRILLED VEGGIES

RATATOUILLE *with* MOM'S *garlic* & BASIL SAUCE

½ cup extra-virgin olive oil

2 medium-sized zucchini, sliced

2 medium-sized yellow squash, sliced

2 small Japanese eggplants, sliced

1 medium onion, chopped

4 large garlic cloves, minced

1 (15 ounce) can diced tomatoes, well drained

3 cups Mom's Garlic & Basil Spaghetti Sauce

½ cup grated Parmesan cheese

Ever get tired of the same old boring side dishes? Well, Mama Mia! meets Mon Dieu! Try this one and give your dinner plates a burst of hearty flavors.

Heat the olive oil in a heavy, 12", deep-sided skillet over medium heat. Add the zucchini, yellow squash, eggplant, onion and garlic. Saute, stirring often, until onion is wilted and transparent, about 10 minutes. Add the canned tomatoes and Mom's Garlic & Basil Spaghetti Sauce. Cook, stirring occasionally, until sauce has thickened, about 10 minutes. Stir in the Parmesan cheese, blending well. Serve hot. Serves 4–6.

SWEET, SOUR *and smokey mustard* DEVILED EGGS

24 large hard-boiled eggs, peeled

1 (4½ ounce) can deviled ham

2½ tablespoons sweet pickle relish

2 tablespoons cider vinegar

2 tablespoons sugar (optional)

3 tablespoons Fischer & Wieser Sweet, Sour & Smokey Mustard Sauce

½ teaspoon Tabasco® Sauce

Paprika

Pimento-stuffed olives, sliced

Everybody loves deviled eggs and good ones never go "out of style." Try this zingy version as a finger food for your holiday parties and bask in the compliments. You can make them up to a day ahead of time and keep them refrigerated until ready to serve.

Sliced peeled eggs in half lengthwise; carefully scoop yolks into medium bowl. Place whites on a serving platter and set aside. Add all remaining ingredients except paprika and sliced olives to the yolks. Using the back of a fork, mash yolks and other ingredients until well blended. Using a spoon, fill each white with a portion of the filling, rounding off the top. Or, for a more elegant presentation, spoon filling into a pastry bag fitted with a star tip and pipe the filling into the whites. Sprinkle stuffed eggs with paprika; place an olive slice in the center of each. Refrigerate until ready to serve. 48 stuffed egg halves. Serves 8–12.

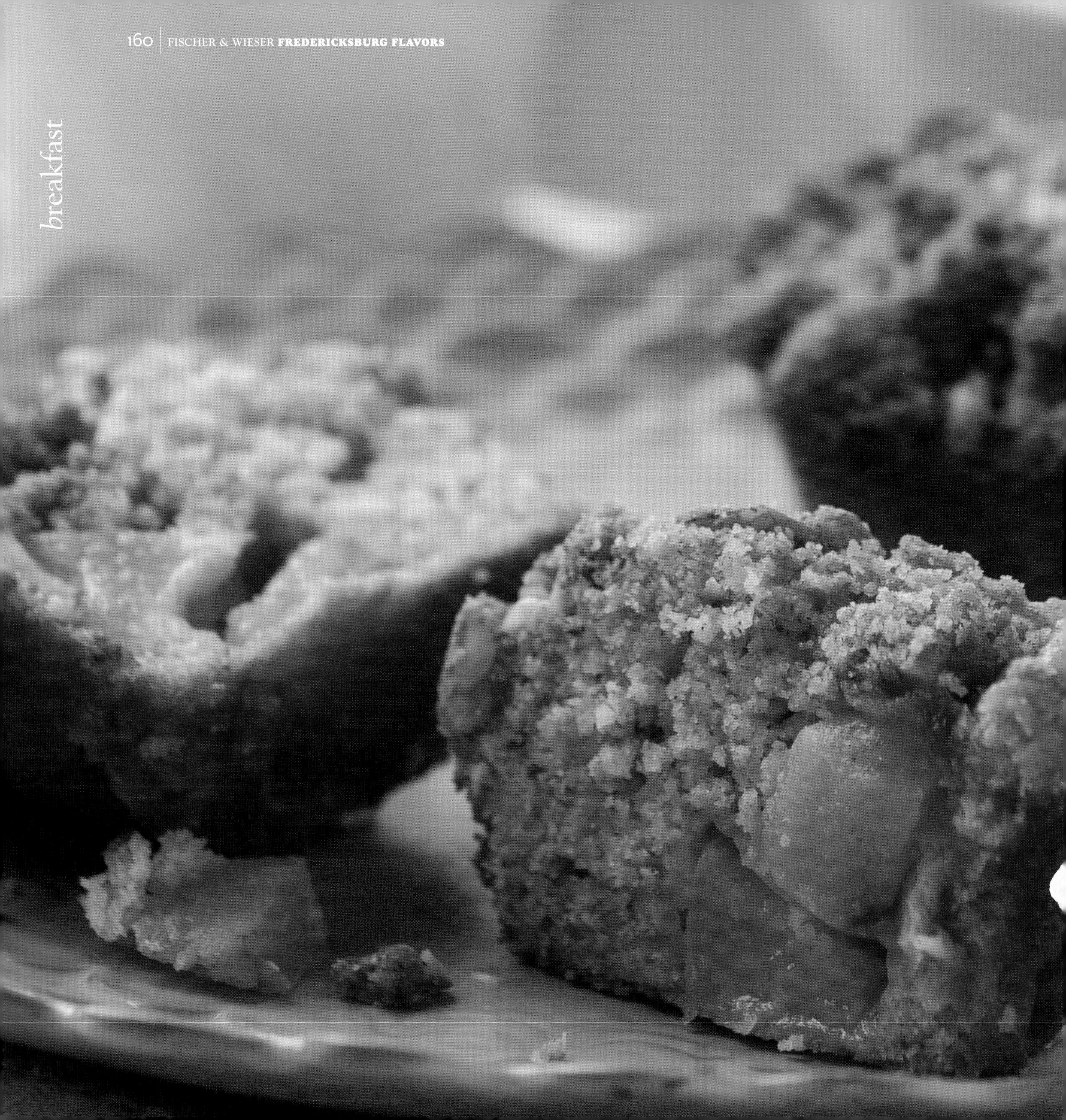

RECIPES

breakfast

breakfast

PUMPKIN PIE *butter empanadas*

1 (8 ounce) can crescent rolls

⅓–½ cup Fischer & Wieser Pumpkin Pie Butter

1 can cream cheese frosting (optional)

These are the easiest little breakfast treats your family will ever love.

Preheat oven to 400° F. Open crescent rolls and separate triangles. Place 1 tablespoon Fischer & Wieser Pumpkin Pie Butter in center of each crescent roll. Fold over and press edges together. Place on cookie sheet and bake for 10–12 minutes, or until empanadas are golden brown. Remove from oven. Allow to cool. Frost if desired with cream cheese frosting. Serves 4.

HUEVOS *con* MIGAS

3 corn tortillas, cut into small strips

¼ cup canola oil

1 dozen eggs

4 tablespoons sea salt

1 poblano chile, roasted, peeled, seeded and chopped

1 medium white onion, cut into ¼ inch dice

1 cup (8 ounces) shredded Asadero cheese

1–1½ cups Fischer & Wieser Salsa Verde Ranchera

When you're searching your brain for a really good weekend breakfast or brunch dish, try this tasty Tex-Mex favorite of scrambled egg and tortilla strips.

Heat canola oil in a heavy 12" skillet over medium heat. Fry the tortilla strips until they are light golden brown (3–4 minutes). Break eggs into a large bowl and whisk them with the sea salt. Add all remaining ingredients and stir to blend well. Pour the mixture into the skillet with the tortillas and scramble until eggs are set to desired consistency. Serve hot with Fischer & Wieser Salsa Verde Ranchera. Serves 6.

PUMPKIN PIE BUTTER EMPANADAS

breakfast

NANCY'S *"Aunt Jennie's"* KOLACHES

DOUGH:

2 packages dry active yeast

1 cup sugar

1 cup water, warmed to 100–115° F

1 cup milk, warmed to 100–115° F

1 cup half and half, warmed to 100–115° F

2 egg yolks

½ cup canola oil

1½ teaspoons salt

9–12 cups flour

FILLING:

1½ cups dried apricots, roughly chopped

1½ cups water

½–¾ cup sugar

2 teaspoons cinnamon

½ stick butter

NOTE: Alternatively you could roll out the dough into 3 (3") squares. Fill with your favorite sausage link and a slice of American or cheddar cheese. Enclose the filling with the dough and place on a baking sheet. Brush with melted butter and bake for 25 minutes at 350° F, until golden brown.

Our friend Nancy Marr, who teaches cooking classes at Austin's Central Market, knows well the great Czech-derived Hill Country pastry called the kolache. Here's the recipe her family loves, courtesy of her mother Lorie's aunt Jennie. We want to thank all three of them.

Combine the yeast, sugar and warm water. Stir to combine. Set aside for 10 minutes, or until the yeast begins to activate. Small bubbles will start to form on the top. Pour the yeast mixture into a large mixing bowl. Add the warm milk, half and half, egg yolks, oil, and salt. Stir to combine. Gradually stir in the flour, one cup at a time until the dough is smooth. Do not overwork the dough. The amount of flour you will need depends on the humidity in the air. It should still be slightly sticky. Transfer to a lightly greased bowl, cover with a towel and set aside in a warm place until the dough doubles in size. Shape into small balls and place on a greased cookie sheet or cake pan. Set aside to rise again, until doubled in size.

For the filling: Place the apricots in a heavy-bottom medium saucepan and cover with the water. Cook on low heat until the apricots start to break down. Add half of the sugar and cinnamon and cook for 10 minutes more or until all of the water has evaporated. Mash the apricots, add the remaining sugar and butter. (Add more sugar or a teaspoon of vanilla if you'd like it sweeter.) Make a small depression in each ball. Fill with the apricot fruit filling. Brush with melted butter or canola oil. Bake at 350° F for 25 minutes or until golden brown. Serves 12–14.

WHOLE *lemon &* FIG *marmalade and goat* CHEESE TARTS

1¼ cups Fischer & Wieser Whole Lemon & Fig Marmalade

¾ cup dried figs, chopped very finely

¼ cup water

2 (2.1 ounce) packages mini phyllo shells (such as Athens)

½ cup (4 ounces) fat-free cream cheese, softened

1 (4 ounce) package goat cheese

1 large egg white

1 tablespoon 1% low-fat milk

2 tablespoons powdered sugar

1 tablespoon all-purpose flour

⅛ teaspoon salt

Looking for a different breakfast or brunch offering? Try these great little tarts with an old-fashioned marmalade—plus the surprising goat cheese.

Combine Fischer & Wieser Whole Lemon & Fig Marmalade, dried chopped figs and water in small saucepan. Bring to a boil and simmer 15–20 minutes, until figs soften and liquid reduces. Remove from heat and allow to cool. Preheat oven to 350° F. Arrange phyllo shells in a single layer on a jelly roll pan or cookie sheet. Combine cheeses in a medium bowl; beat with a mixer at medium speed until smooth. Add egg white; beat well. Add milk; beat well. Combine sugar, flour and salt; add to cheese mixture, beating well. Spoon about 1½ teaspoons cheese mixture into each phyllo shell. Bake at 350° F for 15 minutes or until lightly browned. Cool on a wire rack. Top each tart with about 1½ teaspoons Fischer & Wieser Whole Lemon & Fig Marmalade and fig sauce. Serves 6–8.

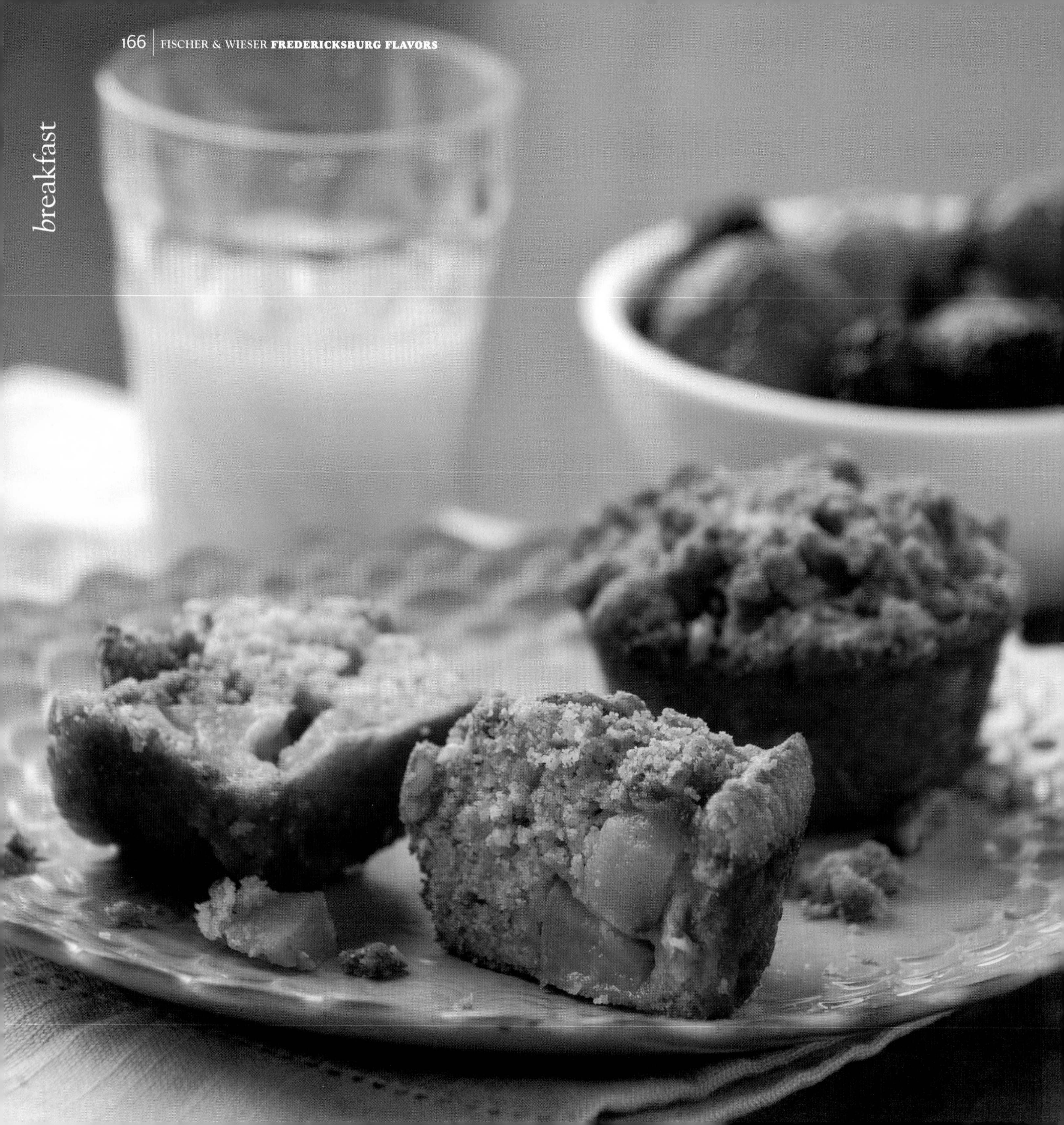

PEACH PECAN *butter muffins*

TOPPING:

½ cup chopped pecans

⅓ cup brown sugar, packed

¼ cup all-purpose flour

1 teaspoon ground cinnamon

2 tablespoons melted butter

MUFFINS:

1½ cups all-purpose flour

½ cup sugar

2 teaspoons baking powder

1 teaspoon ground cinnamon

¼ teaspoon salt

½ cup butter, melted

¼ cup milk

1 egg

1 medium peach, peeled, diced
(about ½ cup diced)

⅓ cup Fischer & Wieser Peach
Pecan Butter

Looking for a great muffin recipe that has all the goodies baked in? You've found it with this recipe. It's definitely a Grab-n-Go breakfast.

Preheat oven to 400° F. Grease and flour 12 muffin cups or line with paper muffin liners. Combine topping ingredients until mixture is crumbly; set aside. Combine flour, sugar, baking powder, cinnamon, and salt in large bowl. Whisk together butter, milk and egg in separate bowl. Stir milk-egg mixture into the flour mixture and blend just until moistened. Fold into diced peaches and Fischer & Wieser Peach Pecan Butter. Spoon into muffin cups; sprinkle evenly with topping mixture. Bake 20–25 minutes, or until a wooden pick inserted in center comes out clean. Remove from pan. Makes 12 muffins.

breakfasts

BAKED SWEET *onion and garlic marmalade* EGG SQUARES

8 ounces Monterey Jack cheese, grated

8 ounces cheddar cheese, grated

10 eggs lightly beaten

1 (12 ounce) can evaporated milk

½ cup Fischer & Wieser Sweet Onion & Garlic Marmalade

1½ cup chopped green onions

1 (4 ounce) can sliced black olives, drained

For a simple but fantastic brunch entree, try these jelly squares! You'll have everyone begging you for this recipe so they can host the next brunch.

Preheat oven to 350° F. In a large bowl combine the cheese, eggs, milk and Fischer & Wieser Sweet Onion & Garlic Marmadale. Line an 18" x 13" sheet pan with green onions and black olives. Pour the cheese mixture over the green onions and black olives and bake for 40 minutes. Cool pan for 10 minutes before cutting into small squares. Serve warm or at room temperature. Serves 8–10.

RECIPES

desserts

desserts

CHARRED *pineapple* *bourbon* PECAN PIE

1 (9 inch) prepared unbaked pie crust

1½ cups pecan pieces

4 large eggs, beaten until frothy

1 cup Fischer & Wieser Charred Pineapple Bourbon Sauce

¼ cup melted unsalted butter

1 tablespoon all-purpose flour

½ cup sugar

½ cup tightly packed light brown sugar

⅛ teaspoon salt

2 teaspoons vanilla extract

Additional Fischer & Wieser Charred Pineapple Bourbon Sauce for glazing

Even if you've spent every day of your life in the Deep South, you have never tasted a pecan pie like this before.

Preheat oven to 375° F. Scatter pecan pieces in bottom of prepared pie crust. Place beaten eggs in a large mixing bowl; whisk in the sugars until well blended. Whisk in Fischer & Wieser Charred Pineapple Bourbon Sauce. Whisk the melted butter and flour together until smooth; add to egg mixture along with salt and vanilla. Pour over pecans and bake for 45 minutes to 1 hour. Remove pie from oven and let cool for 20 minutes. Brush top of pie with additional Fischer & Wieser Charred Pineapple Bourbon Sauce before slicing. Makes one (9 inch) pie.

AMARETTO *peach* PECAN *crumb* PIE

FILLING:

1 egg

½ cup sugar

2 tablespoons all-purpose flour

1 teaspoon cornstarch

1 teaspoon vanilla extract

¾–1 pound fresh apricots or peaches

¾ cup Fischer & Wieser Amaretto Peach Pecan Preserves

1 (9 inch) unbaked pie shell

TOPPING:

¾ cup all-purpose flour

½ cup packed brown sugar

½ cup quick-cooking or rolled oats

½ cup chopped pecans, if desired

6 tablespoons cold butter

Here's a scrumptious dessert that's very little trouble. And it's hard to beat the combination of peaches and pecans with a splash of amaretto.

In a large mixing bowl, beat egg. Add the sugar, flour, cornstarch and vanilla; mix well. Gently fold in apricots or peaches and Fischer & Wieser Amaretto Peach Pecan Preserves. Pour into pastry shell. For topping, combine flour, brown sugar, oats and pecans in a small bowl; cut in butter until crumbly. Sprinkle over fruit. Bake at 400° F for 10 minutes. Reduce heat to 350° F. Bake for 35 minutes or until golden brown and bubbly. Cool on a wire rack. Serves 10–12

Case & Mark winning peach basket–Fischer & Wieser won first place for their peaches at the 2010 Stonewall Peach Jamboree.

desserts

ALMOND *cherry* JUBILEE *jam* CRUMB PIE

FILLING:

1 egg

½ cup sugar

2 tablespoons all-purpose flour

1 teaspoon cornstarch

1 teaspoon vanilla extract

¾–1 pound fresh cherries, pitted

¾ cup Fischer & Wieser Almond & Cherry Jubilee Jam

1 (9 inch) unbaked pie shell

TOPPING:

¾ cup all-purpose flour

½ cup packed brown sugar

½ cup quick-cooking or rolled oats

½ cup slivered almonds, if desired

6 tablespoons cold butter

For a scrumptious dessert that's very little trouble, you can't go wrong with this crumb pie!

In a large mixing bowl, beat egg. Add the sugar, flour, cornstarch and vanilla; mix well. Gently fold in cherries and Fischer & Wieser Almond & Cherry Jubilee Jam. Pour into pastry shell. For topping, combine flour, brown sugar, oats and almonds in a small bowl; cut in butter until crumbly. Sprinkle over fruit. Bake at 400° F for 10 minutes. Reduce heat to 350° F. Bake for 35 minutes or until golden brown and bubbly. Cool on a wire rack. Serves 10–12.

SWEET *potato* PIE

1 (15 ounce) can sweet potatoes, drained

¾ cup light brown sugar

2 tablespoons soft butter

1 (5 ounce) can evaporated milk

3 large eggs

1 teaspoon vanilla

½ cup Fischer & Wieser Harvest Apple Cider Glaze

½ teaspoon salt

½ teaspoon nutmeg

¼ teaspoon cloves

¼ teaspoon cinnamon

1 (9 inch) pie shell, unbaked

If you've never tried this Old South treat, now's the time, with Fischer & Wieser Harvest Apple Cider Glaze along to add its subtle sweetness.

Preheat oven to 375° F. In large mixing bowl beat the sweet potatoes until smooth with an electric mixer. Next add in brown sugar, butter, evaporated milk, eggs, vanilla, Fischer & Wieser Harvest Apple Cider Glaze, salt, nutmeg, cloves, and cinnamon. Make sure that all ingredients are completely blended. Bake at 375° F in a nine inch unbaked pie shell until filling is set, 35–45 minutes. Form foil in the shape of a tent around pie rim to prevent over-browning. Remove foil after 30 minutes to allow some browning to occur. After the pie is set remove from oven and allow to cool completely on a wire rack. Yield: 8 slices.

COCONUT *mango ginger* *habanero* DESSERT

35 Famous Amos Coconut Bar Cookies (2 cups crushed)

1 stick (½ cup) melted butter

1 (1.3 ounce) can shredded coconut

1 (8 ounce) block cream cheese

1 cup confectioner's sugar

½ cup Fischer & Wieser Mango Ginger Habanero Sauce

½ cups milk

1 small box vanilla flavored Jello Instant Pudding Mix

2 (6 ounce) containers peach mango yogurt (or peach yogurt)

1 (8 ounce) container Cool Whip

1 mango, cut into strips

Mint leaves

1½ cups milk

This tropical dessert's sumptuous combination of mango, coconut, and a subtle zing of habanero pepper creates the perfect ending to spring and summer meals.

Crush coconut bar cookies in plastic zippered bag, using rolling pin, or use food processor if desired. Melt butter in microwave, approximately 20 seconds. Place crushed cookie crumbs and butter in large mixing bowl. Stir with fork until butter saturates crumbs. Add coconut. Mix thoroughly. Transfer into 13" x 9" rectangular baking dish. Using small pizza dough roller, press crumbs into baking dish until they completely cover the bottom and sides of the dish.

Place cream cheese, confectioner's sugar, and Fischer & Wieser Mango Ginger Habanero Sauce in mixing bowl. Using electric mixer, mix until creamy. Place on crumb crust and spread with spatula until crust is covered. Mix milk and instant pudding mix together according to package directions. Gently fold in the Peach Mango yogurt. Pour over cream cheese layer and spread carefully. Place Cool Whip in cake decorator and apply to top of pudding layer. Garnish with mango strips and mint leaves. To serve, place approximately 3" x 3" square on glass dessert dish. Drizzle with Fischer & Wieser Mango Ginger Habanero Sauce. Serves 12.

desserts

TEXAS PECAN *apple* *butter* PUMPKIN PIE

FILLING:

1 cup pumpkin puree

1 cup Fischer & Wieser Texas Pecan Apple Butter

¼ cup brown sugar, packed

¼ teaspoon cinnamon

½ teaspoon nutmeg

¼ teaspoon salt

3 eggs, beaten

1 cup evaporated milk

9" unbaked deep dish pie shell

TOPPING:

3 tablespoons butter

½ cup flour

⅓ cup brown sugar, packed

What better way to celebrate our love of pecans than to combine them with good ol' apple butter and then bake them into a pumpkin pie.

Preheat oven to 425° F. Combine all filling ingredients and blend until smooth. Pour into prepared pie shell. Bake for 15 minutes. Reduce temperature to 350° F; bake for 25–35 minutes or until knife inserted near center comes out clean. Combine streusel topping ingredients and sprinkle over pie; bake an additional 15 minutes. Cool on wire rack for 2 hours. Serve immediately or refrigerate. Makes 12 slices.

TEXAS PECAN *apple butter* TAILGATE COBBLER

1 (15 ounce) can apple pie filling

½ cup Fischer & Wieser Texas Pecan Apple Butter

1 butter pecan cake mix

1 cup chopped pecans

1 cup shredded coconut

1 stick butter, sliced

At a tailgate party, just place the Dutch oven down in the coals of your grill and cook before tackling your main dish; serve it up at the end of the game to celebrate your team's efforts. Whatever the score, this cobbler's a big winner.

Mix together apple pie filling and Fischer & Wieser Texas Pecan Apple Butter. Place in foil lined Dutch oven, or iron skillet. Mix chopped pecans and shredded coconut into dry cake mix in plastic zip-sealing bag. Drop in sliced butter (close bag and knead until butter mixes into cake mix resembling uncooked streusel topping). Crumble this mixture over apple mixture in Dutch oven. Cover and place on 5 or 6 hot charcoal briquettes; place about 15 briquettes on top of the lid. Bake for 20 minutes (do not peek!) Blow ashes off lid very carefully to check for doneness. Serves 12.

PEACH PECAN *butter cobbler*

6–8 fresh large peaches, peeled and sliced (about 6–8 cups)

½ cups sugar

1 cup Fischer & Wieser Peach Pecan Butter

⅓ cup all-purpose flour

1½ teaspoons vanilla

⅔ cup butter

2 (15 ounce) packages refrigerated pie crusts

½ cup chopped pecans, toasted

¼ cup sugar

Vanilla ice cream

Fresh peaches and layers of crust, combined with Fischer & Wieser Peach Pecan Butter, make this the best cobbler you'll ever try. And here in Texas, that's saying a mouthful.

Combine peaches, sugar, Fischer & Wieser Peach Pecan Butter, and flour in large saucepan, and let stand 10 minutes or until sugar dissolves. Bring peach mixture to a boil; reduce heat to low, and simmer 10 minutes or until peaches are tender. Remove from heat; add vanilla and butter. Unfold 2 pie crusts onto large sheet of waxed or parchment paper. Sprinkle ¼ cup pecans and 2 tablespoons sugar evenly over 1 pie crust; top with other pie crust. Roll to a 12 inch circle, gently pressing pecans into pastry.

Cut into 1½ inch strips. Repeat with remaining pie crusts, pecans and sugar. Place buttered 13" x 9" baking dish in oven and allow butter to melt. Spoon half of peach mixture into a baking dish. Arrange half of pastry strips in a lattice design on wax or parchment paper. Carefully pick up paper, turn over on top of peach mixture, and carefully pull paper away. Bake at 450° F for 20–25 minutes or until lightly browned. Spoon remaining peach mixture over baked pastry. Top with remaining pastry strips in a lattice design in same manner as previously done. Bake 15–18 more minutes. Serve warm or cold with vanilla ice cream. Serves 8–10.

desserts

OLD FASHIONED *cherry crumb* PIE

3 cups Fischer & Wieser Old Fashioned Cherry Pie Filling

1 (9 inch) unbaked pie shell

TOPPING:

¾ cup all-purpose flour

½ cup packed brown sugar

½ cup quick-cooking or rolled oats

½ cup chopped pecans or walnuts (optional)

6 tablespoons cold butter

If you're into a dessert with a fantastic streusel-type crusty top, this is a wonderful offering. Try it for your next covered dish affair, family dinner, or even a special ending to an everyday meal.

Preheat oven to 400° F. Pour Fischer & Wieser Old Fashioned Cherry Pie Filling into pastry shell. Combine flour, brown sugar, oats and nuts (if desired) in a small bowl; cut in butter until crumbly. Sprinkle over fruit. Bake at 400° F for 10 minutes. Reduce heat to 350° F, bake for 35 minutes or until golden brown and bubbly. Cool on a wire rack. Serves 10–12.

TIP: To make a fantastic bar cookie with fruit filling, prepare a batch of your favorite oatmeal cookie dough. Spread half in 13" x 9" rectangular baking dish, pour in pie filling and spread over cookie dough; add the other half of the cookie dough and spread evenly over pie filling. Bake at 375° F for 30–35 minutes. Allow to cool; cut into 2" square bars. Serves 10–12.

EASY OLD *fashioned* *cherry* COBBLER

1¼ cups sugar

1 cup self-rising flour

1 cup milk

½ cup butter, melted

3 cups Fischer & Wieser Old Fashioned Cherry Pie Filling

This cherry cobbler will be gone almost as soon as you pull it out of the oven. Takes hardly any time to prepare, so you might consider doubling the recipe.

Whisk together 1 cup sugar, flour, and milk just until blended; whisk in melted butter. Pour batter into a lightly greased 12" x 9" baking dish; pour Fischer & Wieser Old Fashioned Cherry Pie Filling and remaining ¼ cup sugar evenly over batter. Bake at 350° F for 1 hour or until golden brown and bubbly. Serves 6–8.

desserts

APRICOT ORANGE *marmalade* *cheesecake* BARS

BASE:

6 tablespoons well chilled unsalted butter, cut into ½ inch dice

2 cups all purpose flour

½ cup packed light brown sugar

½ teaspoon salt

TOPPING:

16 ounces cream cheese, softened

2 large eggs

¾ cup sugar

1 teaspoon vanilla extract

¾ cup Fischer & Wieser Apricot Orange Marmalade

All we can say is....give these cheesecake bars a chance.

Preheat oven to 350° F. Place oven rack in middle position. Combine butter, flour, brown sugar and salt; place all ingredients in work bowl of food processor fitted with steel blade. Process just until mixture resembles coarse meal. Turn mixture out into a 13" x 9" x 2" baking pan; press evenly onto bottom. Bake base in middle of oven until golden, about 20 minutes.

While base is baking, prepare topping. In work bowl of food processor fitted with steel blade, process cream cheese until smooth. Add eggs, sugar, and vanilla; process until smooth. Spread Fischer & Wieser Apricot Orange Marmalade evenly over base and pour the cream cheese mixture over it. Return to oven and bake until slightly puffed, about 30 minutes. Cool completely in pan and cut into 24 bars. Cover and chill for one day before serving.

desserts

HARVEST *apple* & BRANDY *crumb* PIE

3 cups Fischer & Wieser Harvest Apple & Brandy Pie Filling

1 (9 inch) unbaked pie shell

¾ cup all-purpose flour

½ cup packed brown sugar

½ cup quick-cooking or rolled oats

½ cup chopped pecans or walnuts (optional)

6 tablespoons cold butter

When the weather turns a bit cooler, as it does even in the Texas Hill Country, your fancy will turn to apples and brandy. It's nice of us to make those two things so readily accessible.

Preheat oven to 400° F. Pour Fischer & Wieser Harvest Apple Brandy Pie Filling into pastry shell. Combine flour, brown sugar, oats and nuts (if desired) in a small bowl; cut in butter until crumbly. Sprinkle over fruit. Bake at 400° F for 10 minutes. Reduce heat to 350° F. Bake for 35 minutes or until golden brown and bubbly. Cool on a wire rack. Serves 10–12.

TIP: To make a fantastic bar cookie with fruit filling, prepare a batch of your favorite oatmeal cookie dough. Spread half in 13" x 9" rectangular baking dish, pour in pie filling and spread over cookie dough; add the other half of the cookie dough and spread evenly over pie filling. Bake at 375° F for 30–35 minutes. Cool and cut into 2" squares.

FREDERICKSBURG *golden* *peach* PIE

You can trust Fischer & Wieser with peaches—that's how we got our start. So it's only natural that we'd come up with a peach pie filling that'll have your guests holding their dessert plates out for more.

3 cups Fischer & Wieser Fredericksburg Golden Peach Pie Filling

2 (9 inch) ready-made frozen pie crusts

Preheat oven to 400° F. Remove crusts from freezer. Fill bottom crust with Fischer & Wieser Fredericksburg Golden Peach Pie Filling and loosen edge of crust from pan. Remove second crust from pan. Invert and thaw 10–20 minutes until flat. Moisten edges of bottom crust with water. Place top crust over filling. Tuck edge of top crust under edge of bottom crust. Crimp to seal edges well. Cut several slits in top crust to allow steam to escape during baking. To prevent edges from burning, place foil around outside edge of crust. Bake on cookie sheet near center of oven for 35–45 minutes or until filling is done and crust is golden brown. Makes 6–8 servings.

desserts

ROASTED *blackberry* *chipotle* BROWNIES

1 package brownie mix

2–3 eggs

½ cup vegetable oil

¼ cup water

½ cup Fischer & Wieser Roasted Blackberry Chipotle Sauce

GARNISH:
Fresh blackberries

Whipping cream

Mint leaves

Wow! These brownies are moist and chewy—and deliciously different with the added spark of blackberries and chipotle peppers.

Preheat oven to 350° F. Prepare brownie mix according to package directions. Grease bottom only of a 9" x 13" rectangular pan. Pour half of batter into pan and spread. Pour Fischer & Wieser Roasted Blackberry Chipotle Sauce over batter; with tip of a dinner knife, gently swirl blackberry chipotle sauce through batter; do not mix thoroughly. Pour remainder of batter over sauce. Spread. Bake according to package directions. Allow to cool thoroughly. Cut into squares. Serve with more sauce drizzled over brownie and plate. whipped cream, mint leaves and blackberries. 24–36 brownies.

SWEET *heat* DELIGHT

1 cup flour

1 stick butter

1 cup pecans, chopped

1 (8 ounce) package cream cheese, softened

1 cup Cool Whip

1 cup confectioner's sugar

⅓ cup Fischer & Wieser The Original Roasted Raspberry Chipotle Sauce®

1 small package instant chocolate pudding

1 small package instant vanilla pudding

3 cups milk

Remainder of Cool Whip from large carton

This unexpected raspberry-chocolatey creation is guaranteed to please.

Mix flour and butter together thoroughly, using pastry blender or sturdy wire whip. Add pecans. Form into a ball. Break off pieces and press into 13" x 9" x 2" baking dish, bringing it up the sides approximately 1". Bake at 350° F for 20–25 minutes. Allow to cool. Mix cream cheese, 1 cup Cool Whip, and confectioner's sugar together with electric mixer until smooth. Fold in Fischer & Wieser The Original Roasted Raspberry Chipotle Sauce®. Spread over cooled crust. Whip puddings together with milk according to package instructions. Spread over cream cheese layer. Place remainder of Cool Whip in cake decorator with large nozzle. Pipe on top of pudding layer. (Or, if desired, spread evenly over this layer with spatula). Garnish with mint leaves and raspberries. Serves 12.

desserts

AMARETTO *peach pecan* *oatmeal* **BARS**

1½ cups sifted all-purpose flour

1 teaspoon baking powder

½ teaspoon salt

1½ cups quick cooking rolled oats

1 cup brown sugar

¼ teaspoon cardamom

¾ cup butter

¾ cup Fischer & Wieser Amaretto Peach Pecan Preserves

¼ cup chopped pecans

GLAZE:

1 cup confectioners' sugar

2–3 tablespoons milk

¼ teaspoon almond extract

Here's another terrific variation on a dessert, breakfast or office snack. Oh, and it's great as an afternoon snack when the kids get home from school.

Sift together dry ingredients; stir in oats, sugar and cardamom. Cut in butter until crumbly; pat ⅔ of crumbs in 11" x 7" x 1½" rectangular baking pan (lightly, do not pack). Spread with Fischer & Wieser Amaretto Peach Pecan Preserves; sprinkle with chopped pecans. Top with remaining crumbs. Bake in 375° F oven 30–35 minutes. Prepare glaze by mixing confectioner's sugar, milk, and almond extract until it reaches pouring consistency. Remove baked mixture from oven and allow to cool slightly. Drizzle with glaze. Cool. Cut into bars. Makes approximately 2½ dozen.

ALMOND *cherry* JUBILEE *jam oatmeal* BARS

1½ cups sifted all-purpose flour

1 teaspoon baking powder

½ teaspoon salt

1½ cups quick cooking rolled oats

1 cup brown sugar

¼ teaspoon cardamom

¾ cup butter

¾ cup Fischer & Wieser Almond Cherry Jubilee Jam

¼ cup slivered almonds

GLAZE:

1 cup confectioners' sugar

2–3 tablespoons milk

¼ teaspoon almond extract

These dessert bars are delightfully light and flavorful, as well as nutritious, quick and easy to prepare! Great for lunch boxes, after-school snacks, afternoon teas, or after dinner coffee. The secret with these: underbake!

Sift together dry ingredients; stir in oats, sugar and cardamom. Cut in butter until crumbly; pat ⅔ of crumbs in 11 x 7 x 1½. pan. Spread with Fischer & Wieser Almond Cherry Jubilee Jam; sprinkle with slivered almonds. Top with remaining crumbs. Bake in 375° F oven 30–35 minutes. Prepare glaze by mixing confectioner's sugar, milk, and almond extract until it reaches pouring consistency. Remove baked mixture from oven and allow to cool slightly. Drizzle with glaze. Cool. Cut into bars. Makes approximately 2½ dozen.

NIMITZ* *cactus fruit* JELLY

½ ripe cactus fruit

½ cup water

Juice of 2 lemons

½ bottle Certo liquid fruit pectin

---

* 340 East Main Street
830.997.8600
www.pacificwarmuseum.org

In the many years since its founding, perhaps the best-known figure to emerge from Fredericksburg was Fleet Admiral Chester W. Nimitz. The World War II hero is still honored around town for his family's Nimitz Hotel as well as for the Admiral Nimitz Foundation and its National Museum of the Pacific War— created here to honor our native son and all other veterans. In that spirit, we couldn't resist closing this collection with an old-fashioned recipe from the admiral's mother.

Using a long-handled fork to avoid the sharp spines, pick up the cactus fruit half and set in a large pot. Wash with clean water and then drain. Slice the fruit up in the pot and add the ½ cup of water. Bring to a boil, then lower heat and cook until fruit is tender. Place in a strainer and squeeze or press out the juice. Strain several times through a "double flour-sack cloth," says the original recipe. Boil the juice with the sugar and lemon juice for 30 minutes. Add the liquid fruit pectin and boil for 5 minutes. Pour into sterilized glass jars and let set overnight. Makes 2 small jars.

SPARKLING *grilled mango colada* DESSERT PANZANELLA

1 (10–12 ounce) pound cake (if frozen, thaw first)

4 tablespoons butter, softened

3 mangoes, seed removed, peeled and cut into 1 inch wide strips

¼ cup packed fresh basil leaves, lightly torn, plus more for garnish

½ cup Fischer & Wieser Mango Ginger Habanero Sauce

½ cup sweetened coconut cream

½ cup sparkling wine or champagne (may substitute sparkling water)

3 cups sweetened whipped cream

Panzanella is the famous "bread salad" of Tuscany. This creative dessert spin comes from good customer Leah Lyon of Ada, OK. Grazie mille, Leah.

Heat grill to medium-high heat. Slice the cake into ½ inch slices and brush lightly with butter. Place the cake slices and mango on a clean, hot grill and grill until cake is golden-hash marked and mangoes are carmelized. Transfer to a cutting board and cool, then cut into 1 inch pieces. In a large bowl, combine the grilled cake and mango with the basil. Mix the Fischer & Wieser Mango Ginger Habanero Sauce, coconut cream, and sparkling wine (or water). Drizzle over cake/mango mixture while tossing gently. Divide among 8 dessert dishes and top with sweetened whipped cream. Garnish with basil if desired and serve. Serves 8.

The Admiral Nimitz Museum opened the Fischer & Wieser Kitchen in 2008. On hand were (from left) West Point Cadet Brent Carr, Case D. Fischer, Boise Fischer, Deanna Fischer, Winston Simonsen, Simon Fischer, Nelda Simonsen, Dietz Fischer, Jobi Wieser, Elle Fischer, Dr. Jenny Wieser, Stella Wieser, Amy Wieser, Chrissy Wieser, Mark Wieser and Admiral Charles D. Grojean, USN (Ret).

STRAWBERRY *rhubarb* *thumbprint* COOKIES

⅔ cup butter

⅓ cup sugar

2 egg yolks

1 teaspoon vanilla

½ teaspoon salt

1½ cup sifted all-purpose flour

2 slightly beaten egg whites

¾ cup finely chopped walnuts

⅓ cup Fischer & Wieser Strawberry Rhubarb Preserves

These sugar cookies are perfect to make with the kids, or the grandkids. They're easy, fun and, of course, delicious.

Preheat oven to 350° F. Cream butter and sugar until fluffy. Add egg yolks, vanilla, and salt; beat well. Gradually add flour, mixing well. Shape in ¾ inch balls; dip in egg whites, then roll in nuts. Place 1 inch apart on greased cookie sheet. Press down centers with thumb. Bake for 15–17 minutes. Cool slightly; remove from pan andcool on rack. Just before serving, fill centers with Fischer & Wieser Strawberry Rhubarb Preserves. Makes 36 cookies.

STRAWBERRY *rhubarb* *crumb* PIE

FILLING:

1 egg

½ cup sugar

2 tablespoons all-purpose flour

1 teaspoon cornstarch

1 teaspoon vanilla extract

¾ pound fresh rhubarb, cut into ½ inch pieces

1 pint fresh strawberries, halved

¾ cup Fischer & Wieser Strawberry Rhubarb Preserves

1 (9 inch) unbaked pie shell

TOPPING:

¾ cup all-purpose flour

½ cup packed brown sugar

½ cup quick-cooking or rolled oats

½ cup chopped pecans or walnuts (optional)

6 tablespoons cold butter

Here's another great crumb pie recipe, sure to become one of those special family memories.

In a large mixing bowl, beat egg. Add the sugar, flour, cornstarch and vanilla; mix well. Gently fold in rhubarb, strawberries and Fischer & Wieser Strawberry Rhubarb Preserves. Pour into pastry shell. For topping, combine flour, brown sugar oats and nuts (if desired) in a small bowl; cut in butter until crumbly. Sprinkle over fruit. Bake at 400° F for 10 minutes. Reduce heat to 350° F bake for 35 minutes or until golden brown and bubbly. Cool on a wire rack. Serves 10–12.